Portage & Main

Great Plains Press
320 Rosedale Ave
Winnipeg, MB R3L 1L8
www.greatplainspress.ca

Great Plains Publications gratefully acknowledges the financial support provided for its publishing program by the Government of Canada through the Canada Book Fund; the Canada Council for the Arts; the Province of Manitoba through the Book Publishing Tax Credit and the Book Publisher Marketing Assistance Program; and the Manitoba Arts Council.

Design & Typography by Beth Gillespie
Printed in Canada by Friesens
Library and Archives Canada Cataloguing in Publication

Title: Portage and Main : how an iconic intersection shaped Winnipeg's history, politics, and urban life / Sabrina Janke and Alex Judge.
Names: Janke, Sabrina, author | Judge, Alex, author.
Identifiers: Canadiana (print) 20250208237 | Canadiana (ebook) 20250208288 | ISBN 9781773371450 (softcover) | ISBN 9781773371467 (EPUB)
Subjects: LCSH: Portage Avenue (Winnipeg, Man.)—History. | LCSH: Main Street (Winnipeg, Man.)—History. | LCSH: Streets—Manitoba—Winnipeg—History. | LCSH: Urban renewal—Manitoba—Winnipeg—History. | LCSH: Winnipeg (Man.)—History.Classification:
LCC FC3396.4 J36 2025 | DDC 971.27/43—dc23

ENVIRONMENTAL BENEFITS STATEMENT

Great Plains Press saved the following resources by printing the pages of this book on chlorine free paper made with 100% post-consumer waste.

TREES	WATER	ENERGY	SOLID WASTE	GREENHOUSE GASES
9 FULLY GROWN	710 GALLONS	4 MILLION BTUs	30 POUNDS	3,850 POUNDS

Environmental impact estimates were made using the Environmental Paper Network Paper Calculator 4.0. For more information visit www.papercalculator.org

Canada

PORTAGE & MAIN

How An Iconic Intersection Shaped Winnipeg's History, Politics, and Urban Life

Sabrina Janke and Alex Judge

GREAT PLAINS
PRESS

To Winnipeg

Table of Contents

Introduction 7
Chapter 1: Nestaweya and the Fur Trade 9
Chapter 2: Creating an Intersection 15
Chapter 3: An Intersection Takes Shape 39
Chapter 4: Growing Pains 58
Chapter 5: The Depression 88
Chapter 6: Portage and Main Takes Centre Stage 109
Chapter 7: Closing the Corner 134
Chapter 8: Making an Icon 159
Chapter 9: To Open or Not To Open 180
Epilogue: The Meaning of an Intersection 200

Introduction

"Los Angeles has Hollywood and Vine, New York has Times Square, and Winnipeg has Portage and Main," began a 1979 CBC broadcast. "Or at least the motorists have Portage and Main, 'cause soon the pedestrians won't."

After 116 years, the City of Winnipeg had decided to close Portage and Main—an iconic intersection near the heart of Winnipeg—to pedestrian traffic, instead redirecting them through an underground concourse. The decision was the culmination of years of business deals and strategies to save an increasingly flagging downtown. Whether or not this worked is a matter of debate.

In the years since, Portage and Main has captured the imagination of Winnipeggers. Its inclement weather and winds are the stuff of legend. Purportedly, it is the coldest, windiest intersection in Canada (or, perhaps, in North America). Though, as Terry Matte pointed out in his 1979 broadcast, "There is surely someplace colder in the arctic."

Songs have been written about Portage and Main. Probably most famous is "Prairie Town," by Neil Young and Randy Bachman, which acknowledges the cold weather of the corner, "Portage and Main/Fifty below." Canadian folk singer Stan Rogers mentions Portage and Main in his song "Free in the Harbour." In Stompin' Tom Connor's "Red River Jane," Portage and Main is a place to be escaped: "Here I walk in the Winnipeg rain/ Tryin' to get a bus, tryin' to get a train/ Tryin' to get back to my field of grain/ Away from Portage Street and Main." And Winnipeg's unofficial anthem, "One Great City" by the Weakerthans, portrays the bleak world of the concourse beneath the intersection: "A thousand sharpened elbows in the underground."

If Winnipeggers are famous for loving to hate the city, it seems we also love to hate Portage and Main specifically. And yet we also can't seem to ignore it. When there is a protest or a celebration, Portage and Main seems to be the first place we think to go. For 150 years, it has served as the centre of some of the city's biggest happenings, from the Winnipeg General Strike to Grey Cup victories.

Why exactly Portage and Main has become such an object of fascination is unclear. It is not the biggest, nor the busiest, intersection in the city today. And yet discussions of it always elicit strong feelings and strong opinions, as if Portage and Main is some key component of Winnipeg's identity.

And perhaps it is.

Chapter 1:
Nestaweya and the Fur Trade

If we want to be technical, the *oldest* intersection in Winnipeg is a natural one: The Forks, where the Red and Assiniboine Rivers meet. If we want to be even more technical, it isn't a *fork* in the river, it's a confluence.

As the glacial Lake Agassiz retreated some nine thousand years ago, it left behind a network of rivers criss-crossing the land. These rivers served as the roadways across this land for millennia, and it was through them that Indigenous peoples reached the Red River Valley. Frequent floods meant the land was fertile and bison roamed the plains; Indigenous nations established settlements and trade networks that spanned from the Red River across Turtle Island.

The Forks, called Nestaweya in Cree, was a hub of trade and socialization for thousands of years. Archaeologists have found hearths that are six thousand years old, alongside campsites, stone tools, and animal bones. Flooding in spring left these objects covered in mud and hidden in soil, to be discovered many years later. The items discovered at the site show just how wide trade networks were at the time: one stone projectile found was made of Alibates Chert, a type of rock found only in what is now Texas. The exact population of Nestaweya fluctuated as people came and went, sometimes reaching up to 10,000 people in the summer months when people came to trade, celebrate, and socialize. In the winter months, the population shrank. The sheer number of hearths found in the area suggest that people were active here year-round.

Oral histories, too, talk of Nestaweya as a place of gathering. Five hundred years ago, a period of global warming led to changes in bison migrations and feeding grounds—thus changing the hunting routes of Indigenous people. To avoid conflict, nine Indigenous nations met to negotiate a peace treaty. Artifacts found from the early 1700s show evidence of people from what is now Ontario, Minnesota, North Dakota, and Manitoba in the area. Among them were the Assiniboine, Anishinaabe, Ininew (Cree), and Dakota.

The arrival of Europeans to the West had a disastrous impact on the people already living there. New diseases like smallpox, whooping cough, and measles spread like wildfire through Indigenous communities, leaving the Prairies scattered with burial grounds and ghost towns that were once sites of vibrant community. By the 1790s, the Ininew, worried that their reduced numbers would allow the Dakota to push further into their territory in the Red River Valley, extended an invitation to Anishinaabe groups from the east. Among those to arrive in this period was a young Chief Peguis.

The fur trade arrived in the area around the same time, and European trading posts, staffed by fur trade company employees were established along the banks of the Red River. 'Freemen,' traders who had finished their contracts with their respective employers, also chose to settle in the area with their families. Métis families, too, began to establish communities in the Red River Valley.

Little physical evidence remained of Nestaweya as a settlement by this point; the communities that survived the waves of epidemics across the late 1700s had moved away, but gravesites remained. Both fur trader Alexander Henry and surveyor Peter Fidler remarked on the sheer number of burial grounds, and there are accounts going into the 1920s of construction crews unearthing new burial grounds as new construction projects began in Winnipeg's downtown. Still, the area continued to be used as a

An illustration showing Upper Fort Garry
Rob McInnes Postcard Collection, Winnipeg Public Library

trading and transportation hub for Indigenous peoples, European traders and settlers, and the Métis. It was the Forks that would welcome the arrival of the Selkirk Settlers in 1812 and where the Selkirk Treaty would be signed after years of conflict between the settlers and the existing Métis and Indigenous communities. What is remarkable about the Selkirk Treaty is that we have Chief Peguis's recollection of the negotiations and signing, recorded decades later in 1863.[1]

Peguis described the crowds of Indigenous nations, the Earl of Selkirk's thirty canoes and entourage, and the signatories' concerns for their people. Thomas Douglas, the fifth earl of Selkirk, met with Peguis and four other chiefs—Ouckidoat (Le Premier), Kayajieskebinoa (L'homme Noir), Mechkaddewikonaie (La Robe Noire), and Mache Wheseab (Le Sonnant). Regrettably, the modern historical record has little to tell us about these men. Le Sonnat's son, Ininew medicine man and leader Kā-kīwistāhāw, was later a signatory on Treaty 4.

According to a Peguis in a later recollection, Douglas greeted the men down and said:

> Friends I have come to ask you about the lands, if you will give them to me. I do not want much—give what you choose. Will you give me from as far from the river as you can distinguish the belly of a horse? It is to put settlers, people far off who have misery in their own country. This is why I want it. They will not trespass upon or spoil your lands that you retain outside of the limits I have named. I wish to put inhabitants upon it to cultivate the soil. I will endeavour to make the country like my own country. If I succeed in accomplished what I intend, there will be merchants and traders from end of the Settlement to the other, who will furnish you with goods. They will be a little distance from each other, and you will have a chance of seeking out the best places for trading. All this I will do, if we can arrange the land.[2]

It was decided that settlers would be allowed to live on strips of land two miles long on each side of the Red and Assiniboine rivers (about the distance you can see the river under the belly of a horse). Douglas agreed to annual gifts of one hundred pounds of tobacco to each band, and he expressed intentions for further negotiations at a later date. First, Douglas had to return to England—and before he left, he asked the Chiefs to sign. According to Peguis, they first refused:

> We all said no, wait till you come back. He asked us again to sign, but we refused, saying it would be time enough when the arrangement was completed. The earl said, if your names were down, it would be easier for me to conclude the affair when I get back: besides, your young men would see, in the event of your deaths, what you had proposed to do. So we consented. Our names and marks were put down.[3]

Forty-six years later, in 1863, Peguis viewed this agreement with significantly more suspicion.

> We did not see why he pressed us to sign; but I now think it was in order to have us in his power, should he not do what he promised. Lord Selkirk did not tell us what was in the paper, and I regret to say we did not even ask him what was in it. That was our ignorance. It was a great mistake, as after events showed Lord Selkirk never came back, and never completed the arrangements about the lands. Our lands have not been bought from us—we have not received payment from them. We got some things from time to time—small supplies—but less and less, as time rolled along, until we got nothing.[4]

For the Hudson's Bay Company's part, they were keen to see Indigenous people removed from 'their' land to make way for new settlers and merchants. They would establish a new trading post, Upper Fort Garry, near the Forks in 1822 (and again in 1836, after a flood destroyed the original Fort).

Upper Fort Garry was the hub of trade and administration for the Red River Colony, which was made up of fur trade company employees, independent traders, and Indigenous and Métis families. The colony would grow over the 1820s and 30s, spreading northwards from the Assiniboine River. North of the Fort, slightly removed from the control of the Hudson's Bay Company, and further away from the flooding banks of the Red and Assiniboine rivers, a frontier town developed and would, eventually, gain the name Winnipeg.

One of the earliest photographs of what would soon be called "Winnipeg"
Archives of Manitoba

Chapter 2:
Creating an Intersection

On June 10, 1859, there was a great commotion on the Red River. Animals took flight from the sounds of bells and cannons, while residents hurried to the riverbanks to see what was happening. It was the steamship *Anson Northup* announcing its arrival at Fort Garry, able to find a path from the Minnesota River to the Red River for the first time due to heavy flooding. Its arrival was unexpected and "was treated as quite an event," according to Archbishop Taché, bringing with it a new era of trade in which large items could be ferried up and down the Red River with relative ease.[5] While the population of Fort Garry hailed the arrival of this new piece of technology, however, they did not yet know that the *Anson Northup* had also brought to them a man who would shape the geography of Winnipeg: the founder of Portage and Main.

Henry McKenney was born and raised in Amherstburg, Ontario, where he had owned a general store, but in 1859 he had just finished a stint as a merchant in Minnesota with his brother Augustus.[6] According to Joseph James Hargrave, one of the region's first historians, McKenney was drawn to the area by the general excitement surrounding the West and its potential. He figured that success was inevitable with the influx of settlers who would surely follow behind him. "He found himself one of the few who actually came," however.[7]

According to local gossip, McKenney was driven to Red River not by its potential but by a string of failed businesses and outstanding debts in

Eastern Canada.[8] In those days, starting over was easy: ties between Eastern Canada and the Prairies were tenuous at best (Red River did not even have a standalone post office yet), and it took little more than a move to a new town to give oneself a blank slate.

Whatever his reason was, McKenney availed himself of the opportunity to reinvent himself and of the seemingly boundless opportunities offered by the Western frontier. He bought a storehouse about three-quarters of a mile from Upper Fort Garry from Andrew McDermot, an early settler, former HBC employee, and prominent civic leader. McKenney renovated the wooden structure and opened the Royal Hotel, another Manitoba first. The Royal was not an impressive building but was neatly kept and about as comfortable as one could expect in Red River at the time.[9]

That winter, McKenney wrote to his younger half-brother in Ontario, John Christian Schultz, asking Schultz to spend the summer with him in Red River.

The McKenney-Schultz family tree was a complicated and troubled one. McKenney's mother, Elizabeth, had married William Schultz after the death of her first husband (McKenney's father). According to family records, William was a poor partner—whether violent or simply absent is unclear—and the two soon separated. Elizabeth spent much of John Christian's early childhood trying to hide him from his father at the homes of various relatives before dying when her son was around eight years old. It is likely that John Christian spent at least part of his childhood living with Henry.[10]

Perhaps this dramatic family history had made Henry feel responsible for his troubled and much younger half-brother. Though John Christian Schultz would soon become infamous as an anti-Métis rabblerouser, head of the Canada First Party, and the arch-nemesis of Louis Riel, in the summer of 1860 he was just a young surgeon. (At least, a surgeon was what Schultz called himself. In fact, he had completed at most three years of a medical degree.)[11]

Henry McKenney
Archives of Manitoba

Having Schultz around to help gave McKenney the freedom to travel, trade in furs and other goods throughout the West, and build his business connections. In 1861, Schultz made Red River his permanent home. Soon McKenney sold the Royal Hotel and, with Schultz as his junior partner, bought a plot of land on the edge of McDermot's property where he opened a general store.

The structure of the store was bizarre: 80 feet long by 24 feet wide and 22 feet high, with a steeply slanted roof. The ground floor had only two large windows at the front of the building, with the rest of the building windowed only on the top floor where McKenney and his family lived. From the outside, it resembled a docked ship more than a house.[12]

NEW GOODS.

THE FIRST ARRIVAL OF THE SEASON!

McKENNEY & CO.

HAVE JUST RECEIVED SOME

ENGLISH AND OTHER GOODS.

An ad for McKenney's hardware store

Nor'Wester, July 13, 1864, University of Manitoba Archives

A general store was hardly a unique endeavor, even in the as-yet-unsettled West, except for McKenney's choice of location: his shop would be at the junction of the north-south trail between Lower and Upper Fort Garry, and the east-west trail leading to Portage la Prairie. And to many, it seemed a foolish place to build a business. The land was scrubby and swampy to begin with and far enough from the river that getting water would be a nuisance.[13]

Moreover, the winds were strong on the prairies, and this lonesome and swampy spot hardly seemed to afford much protection from storms. And long-time residents were certain that the shop's resemblance to a boat would be completed by the spring flooding of the Red River—that if the winds did not pick it up and carry it away, then the waters surely would. But though the winds and the waters did come, and though it sometimes had to be propped up by massive beams, the building somehow stood.[14]

Though James Hargrave called it "perfectly isolated," this was not entirely true: McKenney's own former hotel was nearby, and Andrew McDermot and A.G.B. Bannatyne, two of the area's earliest merchants, owned nearby lots and had built homes near the river. Fort Garry was around half a mile away. But with these few exceptions there were very few permanent structures in the immediate vicinity, and virtually no other businesses right on the main road.

Despite the misgivings of others, this location had in fact been a stroke of genius: anyone travelling between the forts or heading north to trade in furs would inevitably pass by his front doors. In effect, all roads led to McKenney & Co.

Locating Portage Avenue

If anything, McKenney became somewhat annoyed by the consequences of success. He had built his shop on an angle in relation to the road so that he could enjoy a clear view of Fort Garry from his big front windows, but

McKenney's hardware store, far left, after it had been taken over by his son-in-law, c. 1873
Archives of Manitoba

this was soon blocked by others looking to emulate his business strategy.

That October, the *Nor'Wester* announced his first serious competitor at the intersection:

> GOING AHEAD: Mr. William Drever is putting up a large store on the public road opposite his dwelling-house. [...] It is in a prominent position, and will win the admiration of all comers and goers. Let us

hope that it will also be the means of helping the worthy owner to that independent fortune which his uprightness and enterprise entitled him.[15]

Drever, in fact, claimed that he had had the idea for opening a store at the intersection first, but that he had been unable to obtain building materials the previous year.

Their relative proximity to each other soon began to grate on both men. Drever complained that McKenney had built his shop right on the boundary line of his property, and that the steep-roofed McKenney & Co. building shadowed and dripped on his lot. McKenney, in turn, complained that Drever's shop was blocking his view—and, more importantly, the *road*.

This raised an important question: where, precisely, *was* the road—the one that we would now call Portage Avenue? The intersecting north-south and east-west trails had existed for some time, but they were only "roads" in the loosest sense of the word, both unpaved and unmarked. People tended to direct their carts down the most convenient route, which might change slightly from year to year depending on the floodwaters and sometimes branched in two or three different directions.

The land had once been mapped by HBC surveyors, but floods and storms and the passage of time had changed the landscape and done away with what few landmarks there were, such that these maps were no longer as useful as they had once been. This being the Prairies, there were few natural landmarks by which to gauge location. When McKenney's plot was surveyed, for example, its distinguishing mark was "a post with crockery and glass under it."[16] Nor was it possible to figure out the placement of the road by comparing its location to the surrounding lots. Many of these parcels of land, originally sold to settlers by the HBC, had since been inherited or sold piecemeal without these transactions being reflected in any kind of paperwork.

Still others had built small dwellings without any deed at all; while the

HBC was not keen on this practice and occasionally tried to get "squatters" to pay for and formally register their land, they were not often successful. Previously, none of this had been terribly important to anyone aside from beleaguered HBC clerks. But McKenney's success made it clear that the land in this particular spot had value; suddenly, everyone was very keen to know what belonged to whom.

McKenney had intentionally built his shop at what he believed to be the exact intersection. If he was right, Drever had effectively constructed his shop in the middle of today's Portage Avenue. Drever, however, believed that the road was a little further south, on the HBC reserve land that surrounded Fort Garry—conveniently, in front of *his* front doors. McKenney appealed to the Road Authorities, who spent months evaluating evidence and considering the matter. Old settlers including Andrew McDermot (then nearly 80 years old) and A.G.B. Bannatyne were called upon to testify as to the location of the road.[17]

Ultimately, the Council agreed with McKenney: what we now call Portage Avenue was on his doorstep, and Drever's shop was on the road. Nevertheless, they did not force Drever to knock down his new, sturdy oak building. The council gave Drever a generous eighteen years, after which the road would be widened from one chain-length (approximately 66 feet) to two chain-lengths (132 feet) and the building would have to be demolished.

This matter settled (for the time being), the intersection built up rapidly into a kind of proto-commercial centre—the core of what would, before long, become Winnipeg. In 1864, the *Nor'Wester* pondered whether this little cluster of buildings might become the future capital of Manitoba:

> The question has been repeatedly put—Where will our first town rise? and as often answered—About Fort Garry. [...] There is no doubt that the Fort is the most likely spot, not only because there is already the nucleus of a town there, but because two rivers meet there and roads

> from all parts converge to that point as to a common centre. We see the commencement even already. Mr. McDermot last summer erected a large building near the public road which was rented months before it was ready for use. McKenney and Co. have a towering warehouse on the King's highway—which name will be easily changed into King street—and Mr. Drever has also a towering edifice rising. It is apparently on the prairie, but is in reality at the corner of half a dozen streets—if we can imagine such a thing. These buildings teach a moral. We are happy to see them there. They relieve the dullness and monotony of the naked landscape and foreshadow progress.[18]

It is clear that Portage and Main existed already in 1864—if not in reality, then at least in the imaginations of the residents of Red River.

McKenney vs. Schultz

McKenney was becoming a respected member of the community. He had been appointed a magistrate of the District of Assiniboia (though some opposed this appointment because of his connection to the liquor trade) and, in time, became sheriff of Red River and governor of the jail. McKenney's success was hampered by only one thing: his junior partner and half-brother, John Christian Schultz. Just two years after the construction of the store, the two fell out and ended their business partnership. Schultz turned his attention to his own business pursuits including land speculation and the purchase of the *Nor'Wester* (the area's first newspaper), a drug store and a general store, mostly situated a little way south of the intersection past Pioneer Ave. But some business matters between McKenney and Schultz were yet unresolved.

The battling brothers turned to the local courts to resolve their financial disputes. Despite our mental image of the lawless and wild west, appealing to the legal system appears to have been a common practice in Red River. The logbooks of the Council of Assiniboia demonstrate that

John Christian Schultz, half-brother of Henry McKenney
Manitoba Pictorial and Biographical

residents frequently used the courts to resolve disputes ranging from debts to poorly treated horses to failed engagements.[19]

Even so, McKenney was among the most litigious residents of Red River. He often took others to court or was sued himself and even seemed to enjoy the process. Between 1864 and 1871 he appeared in front of the court no less than thirty-four times. With no lawyers yet in Red River, he sometimes took it upon himself to act as a solicitor for others. Perhaps it is unsurprising, then, that the courtroom battles between Schultz and McKenney as they separated their business dragged on as they did.

The central case between the two was simple enough: their joint business had owed a debt, and McKenney wanted Schultz to pay his half. But McKenney was often away; as a trader, he had to travel frequently to buy new merchandise or to make connections with merchants. His absences delayed the matter in court repeatedly.

The brief notes taken by the Court don't tell us what, exactly, infuriated Schultz—likely it was these delays. But infuriated he was. When his case was finally heard he exploded at the judges, accusing them of allowing themselves to be "bullied and intimidated" and claiming that he could not find justice in the courtroom. The Court "informed the plaintiff that such language could not be permitted and unless these words were retracted the court could not listen to anything further from him."[20] Schultz refused to apologize and was banned from the court. Schultz had brought forward several other cases to be heard that day, and all were dismissed. With a default judgement against Schultz eventually declared, the Court sent the sheriff and two constables to collect the money he owed.

The sheriff, of course, was McKenney.

What followed was sheer comedy. McKenney arrived at Schultz's store and began directing his constables to seize goods in lieu of payment. They started with a heavy pair of scales, and McKenney opened the door so they could get through. Schultz pulled it shut. The two fought, exchanging blows, and finally "after a series of struggles and confused tumbling and rolling over the floor," Schultz was bound with a rope taken from his own merchandise and hauled off to the jail for assaulting McKenney.

In the meantime, Schultz's wife had effectively imprisoned a constable charged with watching over the store. Having nailed shut the doors and windows to prevent his escape, she rounded up a crowd of some fifteen people to break her husband out of jail: "This done, the party adjourned along with him to his house, where a report says 'they made a night of it.'"

Constructing a City

Schultz and McKenney avoided each other after this incident. Schultz built his own businesses away from Portage and Main, choosing to construct his home and shops closer to Fort Garry. McKenney is never again mentioned in Schultz's paper, the *Nor'Wester*. But his success continued, and Portage and Main continued to grow around the nucleus that McKenney had created.

In 1869, Alexander Begg counted the following buildings in what he was already calling "the Town of Winnipeg":[21]

8 stores and dwelling combined
10 private dwellings
2 Churches
2 Saloons
3 Hotels
2 Butcher Shops
2 Photograph Galleries
1 Surveyors Office
5 Warehouses and Stores
1 Tin Shop
2 Printing Offices
1 Carriage Shop
1 Gun Shop
1 Watchmakers Shop

1 Harness Shop
1 Stationery Store
1 School
1 Drug Store
1 Grist and Saw Mill
1 Engine House
4 Unfinished houses
1 Burnt ruins**

**This referred to a house previously owned by Andrew McDermot which had burnt down.

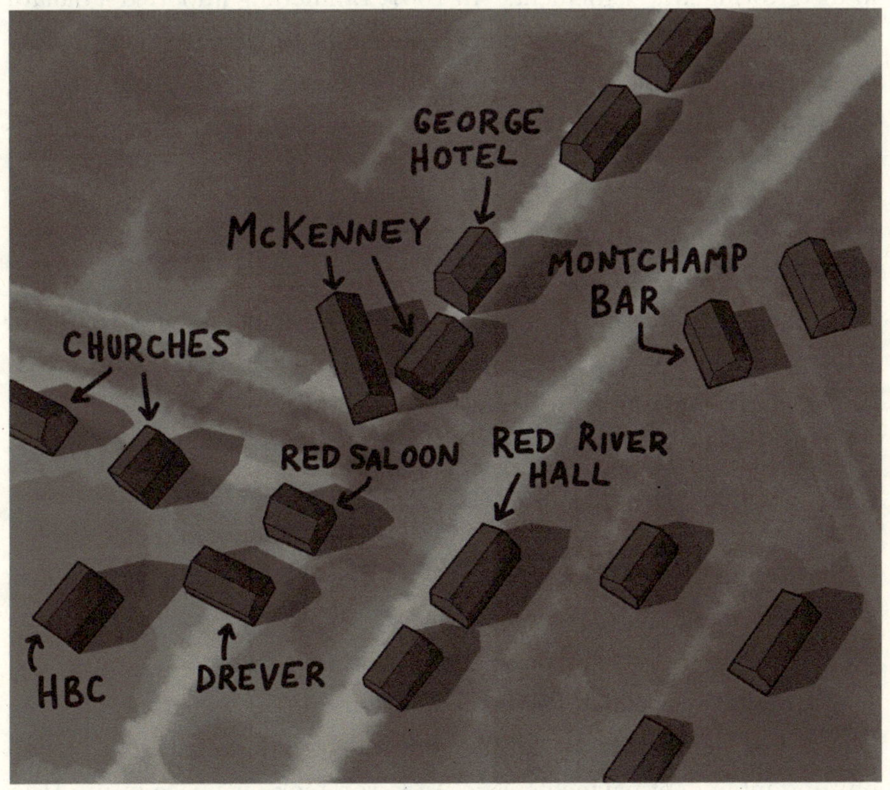

A map showing the approximate locations of some significant buildings around Portage and Main c. 1870

Alex Judge

Emmerling Hotel

After building his store, McKenney had sold his hotel to "Dutch" George Emmerling. Emmerling was another newcomer who, according to local legend, had arrived in Red River with nothing but a barrel of whiskey and two barrels of apples. Before buying McKenney's hotel, Emmerling had briefly made his living selling buttered potatoes from a small shack on Post Office Street (now Lombard).

Sources seem to disagree on whether the George Hotel, sometimes called the Emmerling Hotel, was an entirely new structure or the site of the former Royal Hotel. In either case, Emmerling saw increasing success in the growing little settlement.[22] In 1867, Emmerling imported a billiard table, which proved to be so popular that he soon ordered another. Together, the tables took up nearly the entire basement of the hotel. Emmerling soon expanded, adding a new wing that doubled the size of his establishment.

Merchant Hotel

Of the scant photographs we have of Red River residents in the 1850-60s, many of them were taken by Ryder Larsen. Between 1866-1871, Larsen worked as a photographer with a studio at the northwest corner of Portage and Main. One of only a few photographers in the area, Larsen quickly attracted many of Winnipeg's notable residents to sit for portraits.[23] Like many studios of the time, subjects were posed, either seated or next to a chair, in front of a landscape painting. In Larsen's case, the backgrounds were often mountain landscapes or a pastoral Grecian scene, though he did not always stick to the studio. The Archives of Manitoba have several photographs of early Red River taken by Larsen.

Larsen was also a known drinker, a fact that left him frequently behind on substantial debt payments. Eric Anderson took out space in the *Daily Nor'Western* to notify the public that Larsen owed him 248.60 pounds. Despite this, Larsen managed to move his operations to St. Andrew's, Manitoba around 1868—where he found trouble once again.

(left) A photograph taken by Ryder Larsen of a Red River house and cart
Archives of Manitoba

(right) A photograph taken by Ryder Larsen of the *S.S. International* at Fort Garry
Archives of Manitoba

In late November 1869, Larsen was attending a party at his father-in-law's, Peter Pruden. A night of "carousing" turned violent when Thomas Johnstone was shot dead by a party guest. According to testimony from guests, a fight had broken out between Larsen, Johnstone, Peter Pruden, and John Bird. The initial fight appears to have been between William and Louis Pruden, who had challenged each other to a duel (with a knife and sword respectively). John Bird testified to stopping the duel, while William's wife rushed to summon her brother Robert Ballenden. Ballenden arrived to witness William storming off and caught a glimpse of the other four men standing inside the house. Though Ballenden did not witness what happened next, he reported hearing Larsen say, "If you don't leave off, Thomas, you will be a dead man."[24] Bird, who was inside the house at the time, stated at the inquest that he had seen Larsen holding the gun, though he had been busy restraining Peter and did not initially notice that Johnston had been shot.

In theory, this was an open-and-shut case except for the fact that Larsen, along with Louis Pruden (another party guest), had left town the morning after the party. Larsen would never stand trial, though this wasn't for lack of trying. Reportedly, Larsen had tried to turn himself in to Colonel Garnet Wolseley during the Riel Resistance but was turned away. Following the incorporation of Manitoba as a province, Larsen was arrested at the order of Judge Francis Godschall Johnson and released on bail. Once out, Larsen convinced an Ontario soldier to aid him in an escape attempt, only to be captured again and this time thrown in jail.

How this happened is entirely unclear, but Larsen managed to escape prison and fled south to Pembina in 1871. Inexplicably, too, in the time between his escapes and arrests, Larsen found time to indulge in horse theft and property theft and used his Portage and Main studio as a holding place for stolen goods.[25]

After Larsen fled in 1871, his property was claimed by Erastus Smith Edgerton, a banker from St. Paul, Minnesota, who turned Ryder Larsen's photography studio into the Merchant Hotel under the care of William John "Billy" O'Connor.

Red River Hall, the location of Winnipeg's first theatre performances. Performers would have to climb the steep staircase on the right-hand side of the image to get to the stage.
Archives of Manitoba

Red River Hall

Across the street from the Merchant Hotel was the McDermot Block, a row of shops with a hall on the second floor. This upstairs room, about forty feet long by twenty feet wide, was known as the Red River Hall and became the site of Winnipeg's first theatre. The stage was small (as it had to be, given that the ceilings were only eight feet high) but decked out nonetheless with a curtain and footlights. The makeshift dressing rooms were in the shop beneath the stage, accessible only by a steep outdoor staircase. Nevertheless, residents greeted the theatre's first amateur performance with enthusiasm. The set for the play was the George Hotel, the real-life version of which had a candle lit in every window to celebrate.[26]

The show was a slapstick-style farce: a visitor arrives to (the fictional version of) the George Hotel only to be shown to a terrible, damp basement room. His shoes run off by themselves, and a candle he is given explodes in his hand. The visitor yells at the landlord and finally collapses, exhausted, on the bed, whereupon "the rickety structure fell to the ground under its shouting occupant."[27]

While this comedy was being acted out, the real George Hotel was very nearly the site of a tragedy. The curtains of one of the rooms had caught fire, and with nearly everyone at the play, this would have gone unnoticed if not for a latecomer who saw the flames and managed to put out the fire.

Accidents aside, the Red River Hall was not the ideal venue for a crowd: on the occasion of this first performance, the audience had to be stopped from applauding and stamping their feet for fear that the "frail supports with which the flooring was upheld" would collapse beneath them. On nights when the theatre was on, the owners of the Hall would busy themselves putting up wooden poles to prop up the ceiling.[28]

Knox Church, one of two churches built along Portage Avenue near Main Street
Rob McInnes Postcard Collection, Winnipeg Public Library

Churches

Despite these concerns, Red River Hall was also the site of one of the area's first churches. A group of Anglican worshippers had first begun meeting at the Fort Garry courthouse but soon outgrew this space and moved their services into the Hall. After the building was sold to a new owner, he decided (probably wisely) that there would be no more church services or theatre performances on the rickety second floor.

The amateur theatre troupe disbanded for the time being, but the churchgoers were able to build the Holy Trinity Church, a "simple and unpretentious wood structure" which opened in 1868 near Portage and Fort and also acted as a small school.[29] The Presbyterians soon followed suit and began building Knox Church just next door, though some joked that there was a "gulf between them" due to a small pond between the two buildings. The construction of Knox Church was put on hold briefly during the Red River Resistance but opened later in 1870.[30]

A group of people outside the Red Saloon c. 1860
Archives of Manitoba

Saloons

There were two saloons near Portage and Main by 1870 in addition to the Emmerling Hotel's basement billiard room. The first was the Red Saloon, owned by former Union soldier Hugh "Bob" O'Lone and located on the disputed patch of land formerly owned by William Drever. The Red Saloon was a rowdy spot, and Bob O'Lone was a rowdy man. In 1923, Reverend A.C. Garrioch recalled passing the Red Saloon when he "saw Bob coming out the door in grips with a French Canadian." He noted that the incident didn't make the papers because "we were getting so used to such things ... that they were hardly considered worth mentioning."[31]

Monchamp's Saloon on the corner of Post Office (Lombard) and Main did not seem to have the same kind of rough-and-tumble reputation. Onis Monchamp had worked as a bartender in Saint Boniface before purchasing a small building. According to Alexander Begg, Monchamp was careful with his money and invested back into his property, such that by 1870 it was quite presentable.[32] He was one of the founding members of the Winnipeg Board of Trade in 1873.[33] The few mentions of him in the papers of the time are generally positive, praising his comfortable rooms and in one case his generosity for having donated $50 to the fire brigade fund.

A Death in Red River

In 1869, the Hudson's Bay Company prepared to transfer Rupert's Land, a vast territory that included the Red River Settlement to the Dominion of Canada. This, of course, let loose a series of debates about whether and how the community wanted to join the Dominion that culminated in the Red River Resistance—a topic already discussed at length in many other books. Though much of the drama surrounding the Red River Resistance took place in and around Upper Fort Garry, the hotels and saloons around Portage and Main played a significant role. The Emmerling Hotel, for example, became a meeting place for those who favoured annexation to the United States.[34]

In the 1860s, Red River was a diverse community in many ways: in language, in religious tradition, in racial origin, and in political beliefs. This is not to say that these groups always got along—even before the HBC transfer, the area's hotels and saloons were often the sites of battles, both physical and verbal, over these matters. More settlers from Europe and Eastern Canada had begun to arrive, and First Nations traders often stayed for periods of time around the HBC fort, but the region was predominantly Métis in terms of permanent (or semi-permanent) residents.

This changed quickly after the arrival of the Wolseley expedition, sent by Ottawa to the Red River folloing the execution of Orangeman Thomas Scott by Louis Riel's provisional government. The events of the Resistance also saw an influx of soldiers from Eastern Canada sent to suppress Louis Riel's provisional government, such that people were sleeping two to a room and even on the floor in the settlement's small number of hotels.[35] Many members of Riel's provisional government fled before the soldiers had even arrived. Those who stayed were subjected to what the *New York Times* dubbed a "reign of terror"—a period of several years during which

Elzear Goulet, a prominent member of Louis Riel's provisional government
Archives of Manitoba

members of the Expedition acted with violence and impunity.[36]

On September 13, 1870, Elzear Goulet went to visit Monchamp's Saloon. Goulet had been a member of Riel's provisional government, and more particularly had been part of the committee that ordered the execution of Thomas Scott. While he was standing in the doorway chatting with Monchamp, Goulet was spotted by members of the Wolseley Expedition and fled to the Red River, which he attempted to swim across in order to reach the safety of Saint Boniface.[37] Goulet was pelted with rocks and ultimately drowned. While an inquest was held, witnesses were uncooperative, and no one was ever held responsible for the death.

This incident told the Red River Métis that they were not safe, and the violence enacted over the following several years confirmed it. With little to do after the negotiation of the Manitoba Act and the end of the Resistance, Wolseley's soldiers spent their days hanging around the saloons and billiard rooms or roaming the streets and getting into fights. Riel's provisional government had executed Thomas Scott, and members of the Wolseley expedition seemed keen to enact vengeance on any remaining French-speaking residents. Many Métis travelled west, fleeing this violence and following the ever-diminishing number of bison.

Henry McKenney left, too. He had been an annexationist and ultimately decided to make his home south of the border. Most annexationists favoured this path because they felt it offered better commercial prospects or because they sought independence from Great Britain, but some contemporaries theorized that McKenney's ideology had more to do with personal matters and that his support for the US was due to his worry that his debts from Eastern Canada were catching up with him.[38] His original Portage and Main store was eventually taken over by his son-in-law, L.R. Bentley, and became a hardware store.

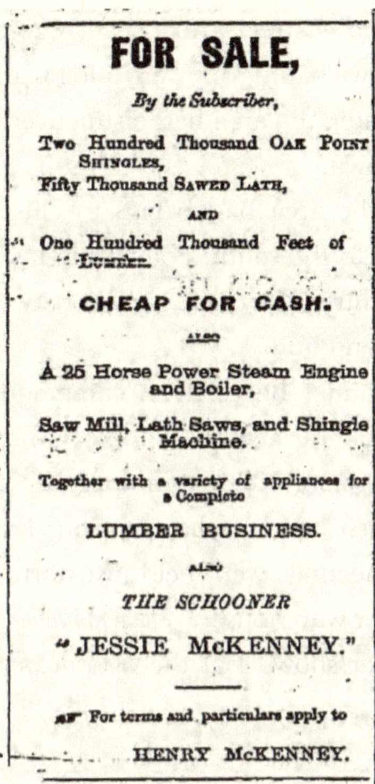

FOR SALE,

By the Subscriber,

Two Hundred Thousand Oak Point Shingles,

Fifty Thousand Sawed Lath,

AND

One Hundred Thousand Feet of Lumber.

CHEAP FOR CASH.

ALSO

A 25 Horse Power Steam Engine and Boiler,

Saw Mill, Lath Saws, and Shingle Machine.

Together with a variety of appliances for a Complete

LUMBER BUSINESS.

ALSO

THE SCHOONER

"JESSIE McKENNEY."

For terms and particulars apply to

HENRY McKENNEY.

An ad selling off McKenney's goods
New Nation, January 14, 1870, University of Manitoba Archives

Winnipeg Becomes a City

In the chaos that followed the Red River Resistance, however, many settlers found opportunity in the settlement (often, it must be said, at the expense of Métis and First Nations residents who had been effectively chased out). Many members of the Wolseley Expedition stayed permanently, and white settlers were excited by the influx of new customers.[39] The pace of construction around Portage and Main accelerated at an astonishing pace. Images from the 1860s show a hodgepodge of log buildings on a muddy trail. As late as 1870, one writer said he "had not expected to see in Winnipeg a beautiful or entrancing spot, but the sight of the western hamlet on that clear autumn evening was a little more disappointing even than the picture imagined. A street with a few irregular buildings, some of them log, with not a sidewalk, unless it were a log with a slanting surface."[40] But a few short years later, the area had distinctively taken on the appearance of a proper little town.

Residents of the area had begun to cluster around three separate points: Fort Garry to the south, Point Douglas to the north, and Portage and Main in the centre. The empty spaces between these hubs began to fill in with businesses and homes.

In 1872, Alexander Begg began campaigning for the incorporation of a capital city for the new province of Manitoba—the City of Winnipeg. On November 8, 1873, Winnipeg became a city, and in 1874 it finally elected its first mayor—the notorious Francis Cornish. Winnipeg's first city council meetings were held just north of Portage and Main, in McKenney's former warehouse.[41] *The Manitoban*'s description of Winnipeg this short time later shows that the overall perception of Winnipeg has markedly improved:

> Although four years ago we were hardly entitled to the name of village, in a few years we may reasonably expect to have the right to be called not only a city, but a large one at that. Gas in our streets and houses, city passenger railways running in every direction, Nicholson's pavement on our streets, a grand central railway station, fire alarm telegraph and steam fire engines, water works, and small boys running around selling Daily Manitobans—only three cents, take a paper sir?

Chapter 3:

An Intersection Takes Shape

It would take forty years, a lawsuit, an identity crisis, and hundreds of thousands of dollars in construction for Portage and Main to take shape as a proper bustling intersection.

While the Hudson's Bay Company was no longer the governing body of the Red River Valley, they were interested in maintaining financial control. When the land title for Manitoba transferred to the Dominion of Canada, the HBC retained a 465-acre parcel that they intended to turn into an idyllic town centred around Broadway. Spacious lots were set aside alongside an organized grid of streets planned out from the Assiniboine River to Portage Avenue. Or, that is, what would become Portage Avenue.

Prior to Winnipeg's incorporation as a city in 1874, planning of streets was a largely ad-hoc endeavor funded by a handful of wealthy business owners. Early debates about Winnipeg's incorporation highlighted the need for stronger city planning. In 1872, Alexander Begg argued in *Manitoba Trade* that incorporating would let Winnipeg

> ...have our streets laid out regularly, so that in the future there will be easy access from one point to another, as well as neatness in the appearance of the place. Now, there is no such thing and this individual or that one can plan a street on his property to answer his own individual purposes, irrespective of the community at large.[42]

While the muddy trails that had serviced the community worked in a fur-trading settlement, it was not benefitting a real city. By 1875, Winnipeg's city council announced $2,500 to properly grade Main Street and Portage Avenue, turning those muddy trails into roads that, while still muddy, were at least flatter.

The development of Portage Avenue was not welcome news to the HBC, who had hoped to turn Broadway into Winnipeg's major thoroughfare. In a legal gamble, they sought an injunction against the city and threatened to charge anyone attempting road work on Portage Avenue with trespassing.

The crux of their argument was a decade-old debate about the exact width of Portage Avenue that went back to the construction of Drever's store. Additionally, in their opinion, Portage Avenue had never been an actual road—merely one of the many trails criss-crossing the landscape.

Unfortunately for the Company, the records for the Council of Assiniboia had been kept. Portage Avenue was wider than the HBC had argued, and generally people considered it a proper road. The judge denied the HBC's attempted injunction.

Road grading and the construction of wood-plank sidewalks began along both Portage and Main Street. The *Winnipeg Free Press* boasted that these new developments would make Portage Avenue a favourite driving road for "high-stepping horses, of which Winnipeg boasts a greater number than any city of twice its size in the Dominion."[43]

What's In a Name?

It took less than a decade for Winnipeg to experience its first identity crisis. The Canadian Pacific Railway had reached Winnipeg in 1881, bringing with it a real estate boom that swept over the city. Almost overnight, Winnipeg was no longer a frontier town. There was a sudden influx of settlers looking to find their fortunes in the Canadian west, largely in land speculation. Near the corner of Portage and Main, Jim Coolican had opened up a real estate office. Described as a "plump, red-cheeked man, with a flowing black moustache and eyes that twinkled like the diamonds he was fond of sporting," Coolican held regular auction sales for building lots in the city.[44]

Property owners had visions of Winnipeg becoming a major western city, but first some things needed to change. The outdated City Hall had to go, and so did the names of two of Winnipeg's major roads. There was Portage Avenue, a name tied closely to the now-gone fur-trading era, and its opposite Thistle Street, named for the Thistle Store operated by John McGregor. Both ties to a period some Winnipeggers clearly hoped was over. In 1881, a group of twenty Winnipeggers presented a petition to the City Council to change Portage Avenue and Thistle Street to one name: Queen Street. Alderman Alexander McMicken proposed the bylaw to council, and by December of 1881 Portage and Thistle were gone.

It was not a popular change. Residents continued to call the street Portage and advertisers listed both Queen Street and Portage as their addresses in local newspapers. It also didn't stick. Residents had grown used to Portage Avenue and, according to the *Winnipeg Daily Sun*, "could not get over the habit, and consequently a good deal of annoyance and trouble was caused by the new name."[45]

When the real estate bubble crashed in 1883, the early high hopes for Winnipeg were dashed (though only momentarily). Late that year, *another* petition was presented at a city council meeting to restore Portage Avenue and Thistle Street. This didn't come as a surprise, as the *Winnipeg Free Press* noted, "the thoroughfare will never be known by any other, at any rate."[46] This new petition was accepted, and Portage Avenue and Thistle Street were changed back in 1884.

For the business owners on Thistle Street, the change *back* was not well received. Portage Avenue had more cachet to it, and even Mayor Logan suggested changing Thistle to Portage in 1884 as the street "was only a very short one."[47] Though the suggestion was ignored at the time, Thistle Street was unofficially known as Portage Avenue East by the 1890s and formally changed in 1901.

Of course, business continued regardless of *what* the streets were called. Main Street would develop as a major finance hub, with rows of banking halls framing the streets, and Portage Avenue would grow rapidly after Eaton's Department Store opened in 1905.

Streetcars

The rush of settlers to Winnipeg in the 1880s meant the sudden expansion of residential neighbourhoods and suburbs, and the increase of commuters who needed to access workplaces and retail in Winnipeg's hub. Early travel was done on foot or by horse and carriage, but that grew less convenient as Winnipeg expanded. There was a brief attempt to run a horse-drawn omnibus up Main Street in 1877, though it lasted less than a year, and it would take until the 1880s for someone to broach the idea of public transit once more.

Albert W. Austin arrived in Winnipeg in 1880, just twenty-three years old, with money to spend courtesy of his wealthy father, James Austin, and an investor, Edmund Osler. He had two big dreams for Winnipeg, one practical and needed and one deeply impractical.

His impractical idea was a big one: Relocate Winnipeg further north to the shores of Lake Winnipeg in order to access cleaner drinker water. The Red and Assiniboine Rivers were continually contaminated by Winnipeg's inefficient sewer systems, leading to frequent typhoid outbreaks. Once the railroads arrived in Winnipeg, though, any chance of moving the city was gone.

Luckily, Austin's other idea was more sensible: the creation of a public transit system running along Main Street. This idea had public support and the financial backing of wealthy residents Alexander Calder, Hugh Sutherland, and James Ashdown. The Winnipeg Street Railway Company was incorporated in 1882, and horse-drawn trams began taking passengers up and down Main Street from City Hall to Upper Fort Garry on a wooden track.

No one would claim the carriages were comfortable travel. Even with graded roads, they were still uneven, and the modern luxuries like shock absorbers had yet to be invented, so passengers were jostled to-and-fro with each bump on the track. And they were slow, moving at a little less than ten kilometers an hour. Still, when driver James Wilson began the first-ever trip, a crowd had gathered to watch and cheer.

Austin expanded a Portage Avenue route in 1883 and continued to expand into 1884. Weather was a continual threat to the Winnipeg Street Railway Company, and 1884 was a particularly rough year. When winter came around, the tracks had to be abandoned, and the streetcars were swapped out for sleighs that had straw-covered floors for warmth. The spring of 1884 was an exceptionally muddy one, and crews were required to clear ice and debris from the tracks. As often happens in Manitoba, the first hints of spring in late March were deceptive and an April blizzard quickly followed. It took a full day for a crew of men to clear the tracks along Main Street and Portage Avenue.

For pedestrians looking to avoid the watery roads, the streetcar tracks provided a drier alternative (though an inconvenient one for the streetcar operators). When Austin approached city council for $1,000 in compensation, it seemed to prompt city council to finally consider paving Main Street.

Electric streetcars came a decade later, when Austin sold his company to William Mackenzie and James Ross, who created the Winnipeg Electric Street Railway Company. The changeover to electric streetcars was slow, and for a time both horse-drawn and electric cars ran side-by-side along the roads.

The streetcar network expanded as Winnipeg did, connecting growing suburbs with the bustling urban centre—and at the core of this network was Portage and Main.[48]

A bustling crowd at Portage and Main, c. 1906
Robert Berman Postcard Collection, Winnipeg Public Library

The Four Corners

The crash of 1883 prevented any major economic development at Portage and Main for the following decades, though one by one the earlier frontier structures were replaced by bigger and better buildings that represented Winnipeg's new business interests. It would take until the 1910s for Portage and Main to settle into the landscape.

Northwest Corner

Unlike the neighbouring corners of the intersection, the northwest side of Portage and Main would remain broken up into smaller land parcels well into the 1890s. High real estate values around the intersection prevented developers from buying several parcels at once, so developers were left to work with what little space they had.

Though Henry McKenney had long since left town, his store continued to occupy the intersection until 1887 when it was replaced by the Western Canada Loan and Savings Company Building, a sturdy brick Queen Anne Revival structure. The tenants of the building were a mishmash of businesses, including a dentist, a dressmaker, several law offices, and an office (and living space) for the local branch of the Freemasons. A disastrous fire in 1894 led to the complete destruction of the interior of the building and the relocation of the tenants. John McBride, the Tyler, or guard, for the Freemasons, lived on the upper floor of the Western Canada Loan Building and woke on the night of November 16, 1894 to heat and the smell of smoke. He had, luckily, prepared for a situation just like this

The Western Canada Loans Building fire was not the only fire that night. Several hours after the Western Canada Loans fire was reported, another was discovered at the Grand Union Hotel. Unfortunately, due to a series of equipment failures, there was only one working fire engine in Winnipeg and the water pressure at the Grand Union Hotel was lackluster at best.
Winnipeg Daily Tribune, December 16, 1894 Winnipeg Tribune Archives/University of Manitoba

and kept a length of rope tied to something sturdy in his room which he used to scale down the exterior of the building.

Insurance estimates put the damages to the building and the tenants' furnishings somewhere around $63,000. Though the building itself was heavily damaged, the neighbouring buildings remained unscathed, and repairs were completed by 1896. Tenants came and went until Canadian National Railways purchased the building in 1902 and transformed it into the company's telegraph hub.

The Nanton Block

The Merchant Hotel, once the property of photographer Ryder Larsen, remained next door to the Western Canada Loan and Savings Building until 1907, when the property was purchased by brokerage firm Osler, Hammond, and Nanton and demolished.

Osler, Hammond, and Nanton had arrived in Winnipeg at the tail end of the real estate rush in 1883, with the twenty-three-year-old Nanton leading the western offices. The company grew quickly and moved three times in the span of fifteen years. When a parcel of land was purchased at the northwest corner of Portage and Main, it was to be the fourth Osler, Hammond and Nanton office built in Winnipeg. Architectural firm Darling and Pearson were hired to work on the building. A heavy summer rain in 1907 caused significant structural damage to the building as heavy rainwater created fissures in the foundation. By the time building inspector E.H. Rodgers arrived, plaster was beginning to fall off the building. Timber beams were braced against the building to hold it upright, though the shifting shattered a large glass partition.[49] Until repairs could be done, the C.N. Railway Building next door removed all their furniture from the west side of the building as a precaution in case the building collapsed.[50] It did not, and construction resumed not long after. When complete, the building stood at four stories, cost $175,00, and had a fifty-foot frontage along the street.

Nanton Building, c. 1910-1913
Martin Berman Postcard Collection, Winnipeg Public Library

The McArthur Building

John Duncan McArthur would boast that he built more of the railroad than anyone else in the country. He'd begun working as a contractor for the Canadian Pacific Railway in 1879 and had continued that career for much of the rest of his life. Along the way, though, he would acquire a fortune in lumber—first through buying the Lac du Bonnet Mining, Developing and Manufacturing Company and later through the Manitoba Pulp and Paper Company. In 1909, McArthur got involved in real estate. He purchased John Carson's Grocery Store and Farmers' Home Hotel, both just off Portage and Main, to build a new office tower. The building's architect, J.H.G. Russell, designed a classical-inspired tower. At twelve storeys high, it was to be the highest structure in Winnipeg. It was a massive undertaking, overseen by construction firm Carter-Halls-Aldinger.

The building's modern steel frame, provided by the Dominion Steel Company, attracted a great deal of attention at the time of construction. Workers at the neighbouring Nanton block were startled by the loud vibrations caused by riveters connecting steel beams, and crowds gathered outside to watch the work being done. At the time, few structures in Winnipeg had been built with steel-frame skeletons—the sheer noise and novelty of the project drew people in. According to *The Tribune:*

> An interested crowd of spectators late yesterday and all this morning congregated in the roadway in front of the McArthur building, for the noise attracts the attention of passersby, and the rapidity with which these large rivets are adjusted fascinates the eye.
>
> Each rivet, while red hot, is thrust into the groove prepared for it, causing small flames to shoot out as it touches the cold steel. Then, while one man holds it in position in the rear, with a steel tool, a second man attaches a compressed air riveter and, in twenty or thirty seconds, the end of the rivet has been compressed into a round and polished knob, which the biggest sledgehammer would fall to budge. It is an operation interesting to watch.[51]

The riveters were not the *only* riveting part of the project. It took *eight* teams of horses to pull the building's 45,000-pound boiler to heat the building from the Stuart Machinery Company at 764 Main Street to the McArthur Building, the process of which obviously drew attention from Winnipeg pedestrians.[52]

Dingwall's Jewelry rented out the main floor of the McArthur Building for $18,000 a year (not a bad deal if you broke down the square footage, a *Winnipeg Tribune* journalist rationalized, as it came down to just $3 of rent per square inch of floor space).[53] Like the other office towers on the corner, the McArthur Building was quickly occupied by the likes of barristers, solicitors, insurance salesmen, and real estate agents. McArthur held an office on the tenth floor, and Russell's offices moved into the eleventh floor.

The northwest corner of Portage and Main, with McArthur and Nanton Buildings, c. 1910
Martin Berman Postcard Collection, Winnipeg Public Library

Queen's Hotel/Montgomery Block

The Queen's Hotel, at the corner of Portage and Notre Dame, was one of the only structures from the corner to avoid the metaphorical wrecking ball during the booms and busts of the late nineteenth and early twentieth centuries. Built in 1879 for James O'Connor and Thomas "Tom" Brown, the Queen's Hotel boasted "fine white brick, 50 rooms, three parlors, commodious offices, barber shop, bathrooms, billiard room, entrance hall, with sample-rooms for commercial men and all modern appliances."[54]

Despite being a frontier hotel, not much younger than the City of Winnipeg itself, the Queen's Hotel was a lasting landmark at the intersection— largely due to frequent changes in ownership and, as a result, frequent renovations. By 1904, the hotel and the two adjacent properties were owned by James Ross, William Mackenzie, D.D. Man and Herbert S. Holt and the men were seeking buyers for their property. Among the potential buyers was the Canadian government, which was looking for a location to build a new post office. This deal ultimately never went through and instead the hotel was sold to the Montgomery Brothers—hoteliers who had once operated the Winnipeg Hotel. The duo bought the hotel for $174,000, at roughly $1,500 a square foot, making it one of the most expensive real estate deals on Portage Avenue. The neighbouring lot on Albert Street was purchased by Jerry Robinson & Co to expand their existing department store.

Under Thomas and Oswald Montgomery's supervision, the Queen's Hotel was dramatically renovated: electric lighting and stained-glass windows were installed in the dining rooms, private bathrooms were styled with stone walls and porcelain tubs, and new imported limestone was incorporated throughout the first floor. An unknown buyer attempted to purchase the hotel for $320,000 before the Montgomery Bros had even completed renovations.[55] This is not to say the Montgomerys were emotionally attached to the hotel: even in 1905 they readily admitted they would consider selling if the offer was right.

Their 1905 renovations transformed the hotel into an "ornament to one of the busiest corners in the city."[56] Just three years later, the Montgomery brothers hired Francophone painter Vigor Rho to oversee a massive interior redesign. While none of Rho's work is known today, he was part of a larger family of artists. His father, Adolphe Rho, was a painter and sculptor in Becancourt, Quebec, and his brother J.A. Rho created detailed wax models of churches. Vigor Rho found work in Winnipeg alongside another of his brothers and seemed to be a talented (if not often discussed) artist and interior designer. He was also, purportedly, the first to drive from Winnipeg to Quebec in an automobile in 1919.[57]

At the Queen's Hotel, Rho transformed the walls of the dining room into local landscapes: the crossing at Elm Park, the old Picnic Ground road, the Old Fort Garry, wild rivers, gardens, and beaches—complete with gold leaf detailing. Vibrantly coloured granite of reds and greens, with panels of Venetian marble, filled the hotel's rotunda. This was an opulent reimagining of the Queen's Hotel, one that ensured it stayed a feature on the intersection well into World War One.

An illustration of the Queen's Hotel, 1884
Archives of Manitoba

Southwest Corner

Rowand Block/Livingston

Alexander Morris, the Lieutenant Governor of the province, built a two-storey commercial structure where the Red Saloon once stood. The building was obviously less prone to rowdiness than the saloon, and the tenants of the structure offered quieter products than ale and fist fights.

Captain Hugh S. Donaldson, a former postmaster and member of the Minnesota Senate, had gotten into the stationery and bookselling business and opened his Winnipeg storefront in Morris's building. Here, Winnipeg bookworms could purchase an assortment of books, including schoolbooks, as well as stationery and jewelry. Evidently Donaldson did well, as in short order he'd purchased the rest of the building from Morris and the land from William Drever. Unfortunately for Donaldson, Drever had never dealt with the whole 'land jutting out into the street' issue from years ago. By 1883, there was a strip of land, about 279 feet long and 66 feet wide, that stuck out onto Portage Avenue, resulting in an uneven and unusual appearance.

Looking to avoid a lawsuit, the city found a compromise with Donaldson, who received $35,000 in exchange for that portion of land and the removal of his storefront. Donaldson would still have eighty-six feet of frontage from Main Street to Fort following the change, so he would not be "much out of pocket."[58] Donaldson would not rebuild his bookstore; he would instead sell to Edward R.T. Rowand, son of fur trader John Rowand, who built a three-storey commercial block on the corner.

The building's architect, Charles Osborn Wickenden, was responsible for a handful of projects across Manitoba during his ten-year tenure in the province. By 1890, though, Wickenden had gone further west to work as one of Vancouver's first architects. His Romanesque-inspired design for the Rowand Block was standard for commercial structures of the time and the building was quickly occupied by underwriters, insurance agents, barristers, and land commissioners.

In 1892, the building became the Livingston Block when it was purchased by Thomas Chisholm Livingston, president of New York's Mutual Life Assurance Company, for $40,000. The general industries of the tenants occupying the building did not change much under Livingston's ownership, though Mutual Life Assurance did move their Winnipeg offices into the structure. The Livingston Building cut an impressive figure on the corner throughout the 1900s into the 1920s.

The Rowand Block in 1903
Illustrated Souvenir of Winnipeg by W.A. Martel and Sons

Northeast Corner

Given the ramshackle nature of the Red River Hall, it is not a surprise that the building was destroyed by a fire in 1875. In short order, a new structure was built on the site, and within a year, Andrew McDermot's land along Main Street was further parceled out. Smaller one- to two-storey structures were built along the intersection, playing host to a variety of companies.

Unlike the rest of Portage and Main, the northeast corner did not grow across the boom period—likely due to high land values putting off potential buyers. As glitzy new office towers and banking halls were being built around it, the Northern Pacific's small brick office stayed where it was—though it did not stay in the greatest shape. By the 1910s, Winnipeg newspaper *Town Topics* was taking the property owner to task for not living up to the imagined version of Portage and Main. It did not help that said owner, realtor James Scott, appeared entirely uninterested in selling despite the pressure from the media. It would take until the 1920s for the northeast corner to receive any substantial changes.

Southeast Corner

When the Bank of Montreal opened in 1913, it was a capstone on two major Winnipeg roads. Sprawling west down Portage was a flourishing retail hub centred around the Eaton's Department Store. Looking north, Main Street continued to expand with newer, taller, and grander banking structures. Streetcar lines connected at the intersection, bringing in scores of Winnipeggers daily as they made their commutes across the city.

The new banking hall replaced an aging Canada Permanent Mortgage Corporation office building and managed to garner a considerable footprint on the corner. The property was a wide one— having 238' on Portage Avenue and 128' on Main Street— and the Bank of Montreal spared no expense to create a new landmark. American architectural firm McKim, Mead and White were hired to design the building. While the bulk of their work took place in New York (including Penn Station), they had previously designed the Bank of Montreal's headquarters in Montreal.

Looking south down Main Street, c. 1907
City of Winnipeg Archives

Both the Montreal structure and the Bank's new building in Winnipeg were inspired by the designs of Roman temples, with towering Corinthian columns and minimal ornamentation. This was actually something of a staple style of the Bank of Montreal: similar style colonnades were used on the Hamilton and Calgary branches, and those in Halifax, Victoria, Brantford, and Sherbrooke all feature similarly classical stylings. The initial designs were received warmly by the Winnipeg press, and three years before the building would open the *Winnipeg Tribune* was writing that the Bank of Montreal was "the most handsome and costly [building] of its kind in Western Canada."[59]

New photographs and sketches of the building's development were regularly published in the *Winnipeg Free Press* and *Winnipeg Tribune.* Of note was the unusual angle of the building: it faced all three corners of the intersection and left an open plaza in front of the building. "In this way, the bank building becomes not only an incident in a long street, but one of the distinguishing features, or landmarks which help divide a city into familiar districts," read a 1913 article on the bank in *Construction: a journal for the architectural engineering and contracting interests of Canada.*

Demolition and excavation of the Canada Permanent Mortgage Corporation Building was done quickly in 1910, making way for 450-ton basement vaults supplied by J & J Taylor Limited and Toronto Safeworks. Four storeys rose up above the basement. The main floor was a substantial banking hall, clad in Botticino marble and flanked with rows of Ionic columns, with private offices lining the walls. The upper floors were the living quarters for the bank officers, with bedrooms, dining halls, and lounge areas. It guaranteed a short commute, if perhaps a little too much time spent near coworkers.

Of all the buildings at Portage and Main, the Bank of Montreal is still the most distinctive. Helped, of course, by the fact it is now the only surviving building from the early twentieth century left at the intersection.

There was no downplaying the importance of Portage and Main.

An architectural rendering of the Bank of Montreal at Portage and Main, prepared by McKim, Mead and White
American Architect March 22, 1912

Through the streetcar system, thousands of people funneled through Portage and Main as part of the daily hustle and bustle. Showy office towers highlighted the potential fortunes to be made in Winnipeg and subsequently stored at the Bank of Montreal. But what was reflected at Portage and Main was not the city as it was, only Winnipeg as it *could* be in the eyes of the wealthy. Elsewhere in Winnipeg poverty was rampant, with families working long hours for low wages in unsafe factories and warehouses. It was a discrepancy people were aware of at the time. *The Winnipeg Telegram* wrote in 1913:

> The corner of Portage Avenue and Main Street is considered by many to be the center of Winnipeg. It is true that it is a great center, the dividing place of great streams of traffic of a vast population, a centre of the city's rising group of skyscrapers, but it is not the heart of Win-

> nipeg. The corner of Portage and Main is undoubtedly the centre of Winnipeg to the rich man, and that point almost marks the northern limit for that section of the city's population whose lives fall in paths of ease and luxury, but the real people of Winnipeg, the people who work, laugh, rear families, carry elections and form the bone and sinew of the city live not merely in Fort Rouge but north, east, south and west.[60]

This contrast between Winnipeg's metaphorically gilded corner and the reality of daily life for many in Winnipeg made the intersection the perfect staging ground in the years to come.

Chapter 4
Growing Pains

In 1910, the *Winnipeg Telegram* printed a list of Winnipeg millionaires:

> The conversation drifted to millionaires. Someone made the statement that Winnipeg has more millionaires than Montreal or Toronto. An argument followed:
> 'How many millionaires are there in Winnipeg, anyway?' someone asked.
> 'Fifty,' announced the real estate man with his accustomed optimism. The musician ventured five, and so the guesses ranged.[61]

The actual number, apparently, was nineteen. Fewer than Toronto's twenty-one by a slim margin, but more per capita. Some are familiar names, even today: William Forbes Alloway, a banker whose wealth helped create the Winnipeg Foundation; James Henry Ashdown, a hardware merchant whose warehouse buildings still stand in the Exchange district; Edward Drewry, who satisfied the city's taste for beer. These men made their money largely through exploitation of the land and natural resources of the West, and some, like Alloway, through the buying and selling of Métis scrip. Many among them drifted in and out of politics; the list includes three lieutenant-governors, three MLAs, two mayors, a comptroller, and at least one alderman.

These were the barons of Winnipeg: the men whose capital was responsible for the meteoric rise of this western city, and the men who—between drinks at the Manitoba Club—decided the trajectory of Winnipeg and the fate of its workers, for better and for worse.

At the northwest corner of Portage and Main sat one of the nineteen: Sir Augustus Nanton. Nanton had the kind of rags-to-riches story that sold the West to so many adventurous souls in those days. His father, an alcoholic, had died when Nanton was a child, leaving his family destitute.[62] Nanton left school at thirteen to begin working. He quickly climbed the ranks and was just twenty-three years old when he came to Winnipeg to open a local branch of investment firm Osler & Hammond—now, with its

Augustus Nanton
Manitoba Pictorial and Biographical

newest partner, renamed Osler, Hammond & Nanton.[63]

Nanton saw a potential in Winnipeg that not everyone had seen, and his gamble paid off. By 1910 he had a brand-new office building at Portage and Main and an enormous estate on Roslyn Road where he employed a cook, four maids, two gardeners, a coachman, and a groom. His six children enjoyed vast grounds with horses as well as a billiards room and a basement bowling alley.[64]

Inequality, Discontent, and Streetcars

The nature of Portage and Main shifted slightly over the first two decades of the twentieth century. Main Street transitioned from a shopping district to a district for banks and office buildings.[65] Most shops shifted over to Portage Avenue, with Portage and Main itself consisting largely of office buildings. Jerry Robinson's department store, next to the Nanton block on the northwest corner, hung on for the time being as an exception.

Winnipeg was booming. Buildings and homes were popping up faster than anyone could count, and immigrants were arriving by the thousands. Amongst all this wealth, however, the spoils were not being shared—a fact felt keenly by Winnipeg workers. Wages were low, the hours were long, and working conditions were often unsafe. The differences could be observed through the physical development of the city. South of downtown along the Assiniboine, impressive mansions were built for Winnipeg's new employer class. In the North End, working Winnipeggers often lived in shabby, crowded dwellings.

At Portage and Main both classes would meet, but not on an equal playing field. Employment offices popped up along Main Street.[66] Men in suits, like D.B. Stillwell whose office was in the McArthur, recruited working-class men for bridge- and railroad-building jobs—labour that was backbreaking and often dangerous.[67]

The 1919 Winnipeg General Strike is probably the best-known event in Winnipeg history. What is often missed in retellings of the General

An abandoned streetcar pelted with mud
Archives of Manitoba

Strike, however, is that 1919 was not a six-week flash in the pan: it was the end result, inevitable perhaps, of over a decade of labour action.

In 1906, employees of the Winnipeg Electric Railway Company had gone on strike over wages, work hours, safety concerns, and for recognition of their union. What might have been a fairly straightforward labour dispute heated up considerably when the company fired the union local's president and secretary after a heated bargaining session and then proceeded to bring in hundreds of strike-breakers to resume streetcar service.[68]

For several days, Main Street from Portage to Higgins was filled with people, both angry workers and curious onlookers. The streetcar service employed only around two hundred people, but the sympathetic crowds on Main numbered in the thousands. As streetcars driven by strike-breakers attempted to make their way down the street, enraged citizens attacked. They stalled trucks across the tracks to stop the cars, cut their wires, and pelted both the cars themselves and their occupants with mud and ice. Cars were pulled off the tracks, tipped over, and even set on fire. The switch at Portage and Main was stolen briefly before being replaced by police.[69]

Even after the rioting had died down, Winnipeggers wore "We Walk" pins and refused to ride the streetcars while the strike continued. "Citizens good walkers," proclaimed *The Voice*.[70]

Despite having been accidentally attacked by a strike-breaker who confused him with a union member, Mayor Thomas Sharpe sided with the company. On April 2, Sharpe made a public appeal to the company after a day of relative calm: "The city will therefore expect your company to furnish the usual service require throughout the city by bylaw. And the city, so far as it is concerned, will do everything in its power to preserve order upon the public street of the city and protect the property of your company." Eventually, he called for the military to send in mounted men, "all of whom will be fully armed."[71]

The military presence did little to quell the chaos in Winnipeg—Winnipeggers, in fact, seemed shockingly unaffected by the presence of bayonets and a machine gun on Main Street. However, two men from the Ministerial Association were able to mediate an agreement between the union and the company after nine days. Ultimately, the strike ended with concessions on both sides: the streetcar employees won a pay raise and better scheduling, but the company refused to recognize their union.

A Near Miss

Dozens of strikes followed in the ensuing decade, reaching a fever pitch during the chaos and discontent of the First World War. Notorious labour activist Helen Armstrong led the Woolworth's girls on a strike, but that wasn't all. In 1916 and 1917, the following were only some of the workers who went on strike or who threatened to: dairy workers, telephone and telegraph operators, electrical workers, delivery drivers, railway employees, streetcar employees, motion picture operators, and even employees of the *Winnipeg Tribune* press room.

In 1918, there was virtually a practice run for the 1919 general strike. Civic employees had submitted their wage proposals to the city as usual in November of 1917. Unusually, however, the Board of Control had not responded. In April, electrical workers threatened to stop working if negotiations were not initiated. Apparently unfazed, the Board of Control hemmed and hawed over the proposals for several weeks before declaring, just short of the May 1 deadline, that civic workers would not receive their requested wage increases but would instead receive a "War Bonus."[72]

Despite the fact that the bonus would have earned most civic workers approximately the same pay raise as they had requested, the proposal met with outrage from workers for several reasons: it felt more like charity than a wage raise and gave different amounts to workers based on factors like whether they were married or single. More importantly, it would likely be removed as soon as the war ended.[73]

Electrical workers went on strike in protest. City council bluffed that the unions were not strong enough to call a larger strike. Almost immediately, they began to hire replacement workers and threatened to arrest strikers under the "Idleness Act," an anti-vagrancy law that the city had recently begun enforcing against unemployed men.[74]

Nevertheless, negotiations were ongoing and seemed to be edging towards resolution when Alderman Frank Fowler, a grain dealer and later mayor of Winnipeg, proposed a motion that would prohibit civic workers from striking. The city's firefighters, in particular, had been having difficulties in negotiations when this motion was passed by a 9-8 vote in city council. The firemen were infuriated. On May 14—almost a year to the day before the better-known 1919 strike—they walked off the job in protest.[75]

Several other unions went on strike in sympathy. "Strike for the right to strike" became a slogan.[76] On May 16, nearly five hundred telephone workers, mostly female switchboard operators, went on strike. Employees of the Winnipeg Electric Company were planning their own strike vote, while the city rushed to find car owners who could fill their place as ad-hoc taxi drivers. The city also anticipated mischief: they placed guards at water reservoirs and fire alarm boxes (causing false alarms was a relatively common tactic to sow chaos and put pressure on city services).[77]

On May 21, 10,000 railway employees joined the sympathetic strike, multiplying the number of employees on strike nearly tenfold. Labour leaders began predicting that this would soon become a general strike.[78]

The involvement of the streetcar employees changed the activity in the city and, in particular, at Portage and Main. The day after they walked out, the intersection saw more cars, trucks, and bicycles than ever before. Many bicycles were ridden down Main Street with one man on the seat and another on the handlebars. The *Tribune* joked that only wheelbarrows had not yet been put into service.[79]

People who owned cars drove their neighbours around, and companies who could afford it sent trucks to fetch their employees: "An automobile bearing the Eaton sign passed Portage and Main with 11 persons on it," The *Winnipeg Evening Tribune* claimed. "In a few minutes a two-ton truck came by with at least two dozen employees of the same concern."[80]

A *Tribune* reporter overheard two men at Portage and Main: "Good morning. Did you walk down this morning?" "I walk down every morning." For many, however, walking was new. The same reporter complained that he had walked from his home in Fort Rouge to the newspaper's office building on McDermot without anyone offering him a ride.[81]

Winnipeg's wealthy industrialists did not seem to realize that it had been their heavy hand in this matter that had caused the strike to begin with. Members of the Board of Trade met at the Royal Alexandra Hotel and formed the Citizens' Committee of 1000, which called for an end to strikes until after the war. They began contacting MPs and Prime Minister Borden in an attempt to have this put into law.[82]

Instead, Borden sent Senator Gideon Robertson to Winnipeg to mediate the conflict. Despite the forceful early rhetoric, this strike had been relatively calm compared to that of 1906. There had been no riots and no street fights. Behind the scenes, civic employees had already been nearing an agreement with the city, and Robertson was able to push towards a resolution. Ultimately the city agreed to withdraw the Fowler amendment, while workers promised sixty days' notice of any "work stoppage."[83]

Clash at Portage and Main

By 1919, Winnipeg's workers knew how to organize. They also knew that the current state of affairs called for something bigger than ever before—a statement that could not be ignored.

It was recognition of the unions that was really the sticking point. Winnipeg's wealthy industrialists were hesitant to grant higher wages, but they were far more baffled and outraged by the idea that the people they employed might have a say in their working conditions—might even have some level of control. This, they thought, was not the way of the world.

Workers knew that Portage and Main was not the place for meetings: during the spring and summer of 1919 nearby Victoria Park, located behind what is now the Centennial Concert Hall, hosted speakers and attracted thousands of workers each day. Winnipeggers also liked to stop by Market Square, where entertainers and speakers were common. R.B. Russell, a major figure in the Winnipeg General Strike, would have a strongman friend of his wrap himself in ropes and burst out of them by flexing. Once an appropriately large crowd had been gathered to watch these feats of strength, Russell would bait-and-switch the crowd with a rousing speech on socialism.[84]

Once the speeches were done, however, and the crowd had been adequately riled up, Portage and Main was the perfect destination for a demonstration. Throughout much of the strike, workers had essentially laid claim to Portage and Main. Both streets were wide by the standards of the time, allowing room for even the largest group of demonstrators, and its central location made certain that their presence would be made known.

On the morning of May 15, 1919, that was where workers headed. First in a trickle—the women who operated the city's telephone switchboards clocked out at 7 a.m. and didn't come back. Over the ensuing hours, the trickle of workers became a flood. Factories and warehouses fell silent. Streetcars dropped off their last passengers and headed back to the yard. By the end of the day, over 20,000 workers had walked off their jobs, with thousands more to follow in the coming days. The mood, those first days, was jubilant: something was finally being done.[85]

Perhaps the difference between Winnipeg's previous strikes and the events of 1919 was the First World War. As historian David Thompson put it, "[Soldiers'] return to civilian life was mired in broken promises—high unemployment, stingy war pensions, and the denial of rights were not the rewards democracy's defenders expected." Great War veterans who participated in the strike pushed the movement to become more active and aggressive.[86]

Many returned soldiers had taken jobs with the police force,

A crowd of strikers close in on Dingwall's, likely in pursuit of two special constables. A man can be seen climbing a car, perhaps the one where "Canon" Scott began negotiating with the crowd.

City of Winnipeg Archives

whose union had voted to join the strike. The strike committee, however, had asked the police to stay on the job in the interest of maintaining order. For Mayor Charles Gray, this was a problem. In his view, the loyalty of his police force was divided between the city and the strike committee. They were asked to sign an oath pledging loyalty to the city and promising not to join unions or take part in sympathetic strikes.[87] On June 9, nearly the entire police force was fired—225 men.[88] They were replaced with a huge number of "special constables": young men, untrained, given carte blanche to do whatever was needed to shut down the strike.

The following day, June 10, a crowd gathered at Portage and Main to protest the dismissal. The atmosphere grew tense when the specials, the very subject of the strikers' ire, began to arrive. The division in Winnipeg was clear: "As the police arrived the surging mass of strikers commenced to 'boo' them while persons from office windows cheered wildly."[89]

What prompted the violence that ensued is unclear. The *Tribune* claimed that it started when protesters attempted to stop the police from arresting an intoxicated man. As another detachment of special constables arrived, some of the crowd stepped in to fight them. As a third detachment arrived, "many more on-lookers joined the fighting." Strikers wrestled the policemen's batons and other weapons away from them.[90]

Fifty men on horseback charged the crowd, attempting to force the crowd out of the intersection and back onto the sidewalks. Three times the mounted specials charged; each time, the crowd would retreat and then surge back into the street. A woman grabbed the lid of a garbage can and threw it. Others followed suit, throwing not only lids but the contents of garbage cans at the constables: bottles, cans, rotten vegetables, and so on.[91]

Two policemen had been backed up against the McArthur Building, outnumbered and overpowered by the mob. One ran into Dingwall's Jewelry. The crowd demanded he be thrown out, but the store refused.

The other man was rescued by Frederick George "Canon" Scott, a wartime chaplain who fought his way into the middle of the fray. Having rescued the special constable, Scott climbed on top of a car and began attempting to bargain with the crowd. They said they would leave if the police were disarmed. "For God's sake men, be calm and don't lose your heads," he shouted. "Keep the streets clear and there won't be any trouble, and I'll promise you that I'll go down and see the mayor and ask him to have the clubs taken away from the policemen."[92] The crowd cheered as Scott climbed down from the car and began walking to city hall to appeal to the mayor. The mob was not appeased for long, however.

Many of the horses assembled were not trained for crowds. Captain J. Dunwoody, charged with assembling a mounted force, had borrowed horses from various farms and businesses in the region, including Eaton's.[93] Strikers startled the animals by throwing things and shaking papers at them. The horse of Sargeant F.G. Coppins, a returned soldier turned special constable, was startled andCoppins was either thrown or pulled from the horse. Once on the ground, Coppins was badly beaten: two of his ribs were broken and one arm was seriously injured. He was taken to the hospital to be treated, and rumours swirled for the rest of the day that he had been killed.[94]

The violence against Coppins, of course, was objectionable; even the strike leaders said so. But the difference in how violence on each side is recorded in the newspapers of the time is notable. The violence perpetrated by strikers is explicit and narrated in detail: they "kick, stomp, maul, beat." The police, meanwhile, "use their batons"—used them how, and for what, exactly? The papers seldom specify, but the insistence by the strikers that the police be disarmed and the various references to "many more injured" in the fray imply that people were being indiscriminately beaten, probably severely in some cases.

The framing of the Coppins incident in the newspapers is almost comically unbalanced against the strikers. The *Tribune* stated: "[Coppins'] sole offence had been to volunteer to protect the lives and property of his fellow

A huge crowd of special constables (left) approach a group of strikers (right) at Portage and Main.
City of Winnipeg Archives

citizens. For that, the mob shouted for his life. The war hero was knocked down, and aliens fought each other to be first in jumping on his chest. It was a picture that would make Lenine [sic] and Trotzky [sic] laugh with glee—a British V.C. hero, being mauled and trampled into the ground by Germans and Austrians."[95]

The *Tribune*, the *Telegram*, and the *Free Press* all ran stories blaming the skirmish, and Coppins' injuries in particular, on foreign-born enemies. "Mauled and kicked by three aliens," said the *Telegram*.[96] "Narrowly escaped death at hands of aliens," said the *Free Press*.[97]

Though articles like these were attempts to discredit the strike, it was probably a miscalculation. Such statements alienated most strikers, the majority of whom—particularly among the leadership—were of Canadian or British origin. Returned soldiers, in particular, resented these accusations. Strikers responded with assertions of their own nationality and race, referring to the police ultimatum as a "slave pact" which "No man, no white man, could sign."[98]

The following day, groups milled about waiting to see if there would be another fight, but things seemed calm for the time being. Strike leaders, at a meeting in Victoria Park, advised workers not to march that day.[99]

Even those who opposed the strike were frustrated by the disorganization of the newly assembled mounted force, who had succeeded only in causing greater chaos.[100] It is almost undeniable that it was the presence of the special constables that caused the fighting that day: the chaos began when they showed up, intensified as more detachments arrived to the intersection, and quickly ended when they withdrew.

Augustus Nanton had a front row seat to some of the most infamous events of the strike, both literally from his office's Portage and Main location and strategically due to his heavy involvement in Winnipeg industry.

The Osler, Hammond & Nanton Building on the northwest corner of Portage and Main
Archives of Manitoba

By this time his sphere of influence had expanded: he was vice president of the Dominion Bank, part of an advisory board to the Hudson's Bay Company, a director at Great-West Life Assurance Company, and managing director of the Alberta Railway and Irrigation Company, which primarily dealt in coal mining. He was also, from February of 1919, the president of the Winnipeg Electric Company.[101]

While Portage and Main was thronged with people fighting and throwing things, the Winnipeg Electric Company attempted to politely ask its employees to return to work. The same day that the papers carried the first news of the rioting, the following message ran in the *Tribune*: "Notice has been received from the council of the city of Winnipeg requiring this company to immediately re-establish its street railway service." The company's manager advised its employees that by continuing to strike they were harming the reputation of the company, which might hurt their bot-

Special constables block off Portage and Main on Bloody Saturday
City of Winnipeg Archives

tom line and ability to pay wages in the future.[102]

Unsurprisingly, this measured appeal to the strikers' good business sense did not win the day: employees of the Winnipeg Electric Company voted unanimously to remain on strike.[103]

On June 21, the most infamous day of the strike, a group of thousands of striking veterans led a parade along Main Street. One wonders if Nanton watched the events of the day unfold from his window. If he had, he would have seen the Royal Northwest Mounted Police and the military arrive at Portage and Main. He would have seen one of his company's streetcars, driven by a strike-breaker, stopped forcibly by the crowd and pushed onto its side. He would have seen the police and military descend on the crowd with bats and guns, resulting in the deaths of two people.[104] In the following hours, he would have watched as the authorities worked to cordon off access to Portage and Main.[105]

Life by Permission of the Profiteers

During the First World War, Nanton had devoted himself to supporting the war effort and the families of soldiers. He donated thousands of dollars to the Red Cross, converted much of his sprawling lawn into a vegetable garden, and even turned his summer home at Lake of the Woods into a hospital for injured soldiers.[106] On one occasion, he got a call in the middle of the night from an army wife whose child had fallen ill. Rather than call on one of the hired help, Nanton himself drove through a winter storm to fetch a doctor for the child.[107] This was the role that men like Sir Augustus Nanton saw for themselves: to lead, to guide, to give—often generously. But not to bargain—not to be controlled.

Nanton was about as sympathetic a figure as a magnate could be. But even he could not see past his class, and as such could not abide the strike. Whether Nanton was a member of the infamous Citizen's Committee of 1000, a group of businessmen who worked to shut down the strike, is a matter of debate. What is certainly true is that he attempted to use his influence to stop the strikers. In private he wrote to Ottawa, suggesting that all strikers and strike sympathizers ought to either be conscripted or sent to jail.[108]

In public Nanton was more reticent, saying only that out of a concern for women and children he hoped there would be no rioting. Even this was enough to earn the ire of the *Western Labor News*: "Did this lordly knight have such compassion for women and children when the price of coal was soaring last winter?"[109]

Nanton's prominent position in the coal industry made him a target during this time when many Winnipeggers still used coal to heat their homes. When the Citizens' Committee began to argue that the Strike Committee had taken too much power for itself by allowing certain businesses to remain open, with signs indicating as much, the *Western Labor News* printed the following poem:

"Open by permission of the Strike Committee;"
Oh, what an outrage that an entire city
Bread and milk and water, and entertainment get,
Only by permission of the 'Soviet.'
Labor run by Rabid Reds; getting very cheeky;
Too many aliens talking Bolsheviki.
Let Law and Order be maintained! Uphold the
Constitution!
Sound a call for volunteers to stop the Revolution!
Such are the ravings of the scab-sheet 'Citizen'
Conveniently forgetting that for most of men
Food and clothes and shelter to them and theirs
come through
Only be permission of the owning Few.
Bread by permission of the likes of Ed Parnell;
Bacon by permission of Sir Joe Flavelle;
Coal by permission of Nanton the August;

Reinhold Milk by permission of the Creamery Trust.
Shelter by permission of the lumber rings;
Clothing by permission of the cotton kings;
Land by permission of the C.P.R. and peers;
Life by permission of the profiteers.[110]

Many workers, particularly returned soldiers, had also come to resent the paternalistic attitude of businessmen like Augustus Nanton. *The Western Labor News* reprinted a portion of a letter received by a returned soldier who had lost his leg. Nanton responded:

> In your case, I have no doubt that, in addition to your salary, you are receiving some partial disability allowance from the government, which, I sincerely trust, together with your salary, brings in to you an income which will enable you to live.
> Yours truly,
> (Signed) A.M. NANTON[111]

Nanton was out of touch. The pension soldiers received was not only not enough to live—it was "a positive insult." "The letter needs no comment," said the *Labor News*. "One such letter is sufficient to do its work with any soldier."[112]

As Nanton's granddaughter put it in an interview for an oral history project:

> After the First World War he really didn't seem to understand the feelings of the returned soldiers. He expected them to fit back into the slot and he was rather unpopular during the time of the general strike... he was brought up in an age when everyone knew their place...it was the duty of those with money to help those who hadn't got money, but everyone had their position and duties in life and I don't imagine he realized...what the men in the trenches had gone through and how different they were when they came back.[113]

In the same interview, Nanton's son, Paul, remembered the strike as a frightening time. His father had swapped out his shiny car for a less notable one and had sent Paul's mother and sisters away to stay with friends.[114] The family's barn at Rosser was burned down, killing twenty of their horses; whether this was related to the strike is unknown. Nanton and his staff took turns patrolling the Winnipeg estate.[115]

Paul even claimed that his father had been attacked and threatened at a mass meeting.[116] A physical attack upon one of Winnipeg's most prominent businessmen would almost certainly have made the papers, but no trace of this incident can be found. Regardless of whether the attack happened, however, its retelling through Nanton's son holds an emotional truth: wealthy men like Nanton felt betrayed, confused, and afraid.

A friend of Nanton's who wrote a glowing biography of the man in 1931 recalled that Nanton was sensitive to what he saw as betrayal: "You don't know how it hurts!" he reportedly told a friend.[117]

Although the strike ended soon after the events of June 21 with few wins for workers, it had caused an upheaval in the relationship between employees and employers in Winnipeg.

Augustus Nanton's grand estate, known as "Kilmorie"
Archives of Manitoba

After the Fighting

Winnipeg held grudges for many years after the strike. City Council would be split between Labour aldermen and Citizens Committee aldermen for decades. And many began to blame the strike for a serious economic downturn occurring around this time. In truth—as many Winnipeg history buffs know—the seeds of this recession had been planted years before, in 1914, with the opening of the Panama Canal. Winnipeg had once been the thoroughfare through which goods made their way to Western Canada. With the inception of the canal, Winnipeg's loss was Vancouver's gain. Though the effects were not felt immediately, Winnipeg would never again boom as it had in the first years of the twentieth century.

During the war, wheat prices had been regulated by the government. In 1920, grain buying moved back to the Grain Exchange on Lombard. In addition to the loss of price regulation, other factors combined to affect grain prices. Europe, devastated by the war, could no longer afford to import wheat. And countries that had had to stop exports during the war were back up and running. There were fewer customers and greater supply, and the effect was felt almost immediately.[118] In the summer of 1920 wheat had been selling for $2.85; by 1921, the price had plummeted to just over $0.80.[119] Prices did not fully recover until around 1924.[120] The impact of these various factors was that Winnipeg was in a sort of preview of the Great Depression during the early 1920s, with consistently high rates of unemployment.

So, Canada did not "roar" like the United States did in the 1920s. In fact, most pop culture depictions of the 1920s do not apply to life in Winnipeg. While hemlines did get shorter, we had few jazzy speakeasies and no equivalent to Al Capone (though some Manitobans did make money driving booze across the border)—Prohibition had been our own choice and ended around 1922/23.[121]

The war was still top of mind during this period. In June 1920, thousands attended the unveiling of a temporary concrete cenotaph in front of the Bank of Montreal Building at Portage and Main. Mrs. A. Code, president of the Women's Canadian Club, pulled the cord to reveal the monument: "Here in this busy spot of our city's thoroughfare, [the cenotaph] reminds us of the numerous crosses in the many quiet corners far across the seas. Our fondest hope is that it may meet with the same deep reverence that surrounds the one standing in Whitehall, London, and that in this city it may be a solace to many lonely hearts and an inspiration to all."[122] Code's only son, Edward, had died in the war.

The goal of the Women's Canadian Club was to eventually erect a permanent cenotaph in granite or marble. In 1923, however, the Bank of Montreal decided to erect their own memorial "to honor and perpetuate the memory of the members of the bank's staff who gave their lives in defence of the Empire during the great war."[123] Members of the women's club picked up the wreaths that were lying at the foot of the cenotaph—it had been the site of many memorial services and parades in its three years at the corner—and workmen proceeded to dismantle the monument.

The unveiling ceremony for this new monument was small but intimate, with the bank manager, A.F.D MacGachen, addressing the next-of-kin of several fallen soldiers: "To the glorious memory of those members of our western staff who went forth so willingly to fight for their country in the great war of 1914-1918, we today solemnly dedicate this memorial, erected by the Bank of Montreal, to stand for all time a silent tribute to those who will not return." Fifty-three men from the Winnipeg office had gone to war, of whom nine had died.[124]

MacGachen commented on the relevance of the statue's spot at Portage and Main to Winnipeg's wartime memories: "We can all recall the marching of the troops, the Victory bond campaign, the Christmas tree for soldiers' dependents, and after the armistice, the cenotaph with its many services."[125]

The destruction of the temporary cenotaph seemed to jolt Winnipeg into action and brought the idea of a permanent one back into the news. City council appointed a Cenotaph Committee to determine the design of the cenotaph and where it would go. The question of location was not

Portage and Main seen from the steps of the Bank of Montreal. The BMO's war memorial statue can be seen on the left.
Rob McInness Postcard Collection, Winnipeg Public Library

as easy as it would seem; the committee spent many hours debating the merits of various locations. Although the Bank of Montreal location was no longer available, Portage and Main was still one of the frontrunners, along with City Hall Square or the Legislative grounds.

In 1925, the Cenotaph Committee launched a design competition. Some fifty entries were submitted from across Canada and were evaluated by five judges. Just before Christmas, the committee announced that the winning design had come from Toronto architect Emanual Hahn. Hahn's design included both traditional and more artistic elements. The central design was classic and box-shaped, but each end of the cenotaph featured a sculpture of a woman, one representing sacrifice and the other representing service. Torches would also be sculpted near the top of each side. The judges were unanimous in declaring Hahn the winner: "The sentiment is simply and directly expressed in a manner about which no doubt can be felt and no questions need to be asked."[126]

Soon, however, several groups began protesting Hahn's win. Not because of his design, which faced little criticism, but because of his national origins: Emanuel Hahn had been born in Germany. Despite the fact that he had immigrated to Canada at just seven years old and was a Canadian citizen, they argued that it "was quite wrong to allow the monument to be designed by a descendant of those who brought the war upon Canada."[127]

The Board of Trade, Daughters of the Empire, Amputations' Association, Kiwanis Club, and several other local groups sent representatives to meet with the committee to protest the decision. The president of the Board of Trade suggested that Hahn be given the prize but his contract be cancelled, and that the contest be reopened, now restricted to only British- and Canadian-born artists. "There was no complaint against Mr. Hahn as an individual, said Mr. Parker. However, the naturalization of an individual didn't make him a Canadian in the true sense of the word. It didn't instil into him ideals of British justice."[128]

J. Coslick, representing foreign-born veterans, turned Parker's argument against him. Foreign-born soldiers, he said, "heard a good deal about British fair play, and there was a splendid opportunity to demonstrate it." To T.M. Downing, however, representing disabled veterans, it was black and white: "it was a question either of discriminating against Mr. Hahn or against the 45,000 men who died in the war." Mr. Cox, of the Travellers' Association, was even more vociferous: "I would feel like spitting on the monument in contempt if Mr. Hahn erected it."[129]

More than a question of design, the cenotaph had become a debate over what it really meant to be Canadian in the shadow of war. Though the groups protesting Hahn's design balked at suggestions that they were categorizing some people as second-class citizens, it is hard to see their arguments in any other way. Evidently, to many British-born Canadians, citizenship was not enough—people born outside of the Commonwealth were simply not quite as Canadian as *they* were.

Richard Deans Waugh, the chairman of the committee, defended the choice. Restricting the competition to British- or Canadian-born artists would have excluded submissions from two local artists born in the United States and France, respectively, which no one seemed to be suggesting.[130] Eventually, however, he bowed to the pressure and cancelled Hahn's contract. Waugh did not, of course, tell Hahn the real reason. In a letter to Hahn, the committee secretary informed the sculptor that the committee had decided to change the location for the memorial and that this therefore necessitated a new design—thanking him, nevertheless, for the excellence of his work.[131] Hahn requested that his model and photographs be returned to him.[132]

It took nearly another year before another winner was chosen. This time the prize went to Elizabeth Wood, also of Toronto, but a native-born Canadian of Irish descent. Elizabeth Wood herself could not be objected to, surely, except for one thing: she was Hahn's wife, a fact discovered belatedly by the judges.

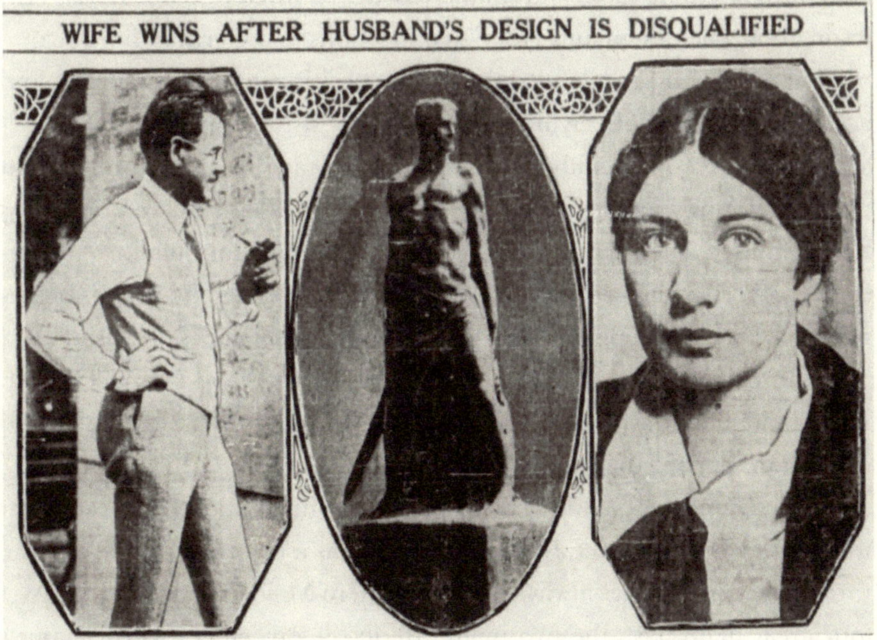
WIFE WINS AFTER HUSBAND'S DESIGN IS DISQUALIFIED

Elizabeth Wood (right), her cenotaph design (centre), and husband Emanuel Hahn (left). Wood's proposed statue may have been deemed too risqué for a war memorial.
Winnipeg Tribune, November 14, 1927, University of Manitoba Digital Collections

Aside from the fact that Wood had submitted under her maiden name, this was not an attempt at trickery or to submit her husband's work as her own. Wood was a respected sculptor in her own right and showed Toronto reporters their separate studios as proof of their individual practices. But many felt tricked: "Miss Wood is Mrs. Hahn and City Hall Officials Are Flabbergasted," proclaimed the *Tribune*.[133] The matter had become almost comic. "There's a jinx somewhere in the cenotaph competition alright," said one alderman.[134]

Additionally, many took issue with Wood's design. It was an unusual and modern take on a cenotaph, which are most frequently constructed in the shape of a tomb, obelisk, or pillar. Wood's design would have a broad stone base rising at an angle, atop which would stand a man dressed in only a loincloth, holding a sword.[135] "I don't think the design is a suitable one at all," said Alderman Davidson. "My own idea would be to erect a column, something plain and simple." Letters poured into the *Tribune* criticizing both the design and Wood's connections to a German-born man.

Some, of course, defended the design, praising it for its originality and accusing Winnipeg of relying too heavily on existing formulas.[136] The design "fairly breathed youth and illustrated the cause that was preached at every recruiting meeting," said one such writer. "Thank heaven there was no committee when the Golden Boy on the parliament buildings was installed, otherwise he would probably be wearing overalls and a cow's breakfast as a more "appropriate" garb for gathering his one sheaf of wheat."[137]

The combination of the public outcry over Wood's connection to Hahn and the controversial design, however, pushed the committee to once again discard the winning design.

And Winnipeggers were still, somehow, arguing about where it ought to go. Many still favoured Portage and Main as a central location and one through which parades always passed: "Where Main St. And Portage Ave. (our great highways), the two main arteries of our city cross each other, and which for all time will remain the centre of the financial, the grain and the wholesale interests, and from which Portage Ave., the leading retail street, branches off, is without question the centre of Winnipeg."[138] More

The final cenotaph designed by Gilbert Parfitt, located on Memorial Boulevard
City of Winnipeg Archives

practical voices pointed out that putting a huge obelisk in the intersection would cause serious traffic problems, a point of view that—after literal years of debate—eventually won out.

Beleaguered and unwilling to run yet another competition, the committee awarded the contract to Gilbert Parfitt, a Winnipeg-based architect who had won third prize. Parfitt was Winnipeg-based, had been born in England, and presumably was not married to anyone whom the Board of Trade found to be un-Canadian. His design was also more traditional than Wood's had been. This, fortunately, ended the controversy. On Armistice Day in 1928, eight years after the first temporary cenotaph had been erected and five years after it had been dismantled, the new permanent cenotaph was unveiled on Memorial Boulevard, where it still stands today.[139]

The Daylight Tour

In 1924, Winnipeg celebrated the fiftieth anniversary of its first municipal election. In a celebration that spread across the city on June 18, Winnipeggers attended concerts, banquets, sports tournaments, and capped off the night with dancing in Market Square. The high point of the day, however, was the parade: "there was endless talk of floats and teams. Every float apparently is going to carry off the first prize and every team of horses is going to be the best decorated that the streets of Winnipeg ever saw."[140]

Winnipeg reminisced about its not-so-distant past, holding banquets for "old timers." But even as they became nostalgic, they celebrated the modernization of the city and the beginning of a new technological era. The floats that passed through the heart of Winnipeg offer a glimpse into what citizens found important at that time. Several floats celebrated advances in public health. One read "Winnipeg—A City with the Aseptic Conscience. Not the fearsome days of supposed air infection. Better than a germ-proof fence is cleanliness and common sense."[141] The telephone system and new hydroelectric plants also featured on floats, as did Winnipeg's parks.

Winnipeg's 50th anniversary parade passes by Portage and Main as onlookers crowd along Main Street.
City of Winnipeg Archives

A handbook accompanying the jubilee bragged about these advances. "Winnipeg is one of the best lighted cities on this continent," it boasted. Winnipeg had paved roads and sidewalks, public schools, police, steam heating, and public transportation.[142] Despite the ill fortunes of the previous several years, Winnipeg was modernizing quickly and was determined to become a thriving hub of global trade. And as Winnipeg's economic condition improved somewhat over the second half of the twentieth century, new mayor Ralph Webb also tried to boost Winnipeg's prospects as a tourist destination by capitalizing on the growing availability of cars.

At 3 a.m. on May 15, 1925, the mayor had a very early breakfast in the Childs Restaurant on the northwest corner of Portage and Main.[143] Formerly the McArthur Building and the site of Dingwall's Jewelry, the block had been purchased by the Childs Restaurant Company after the death of John McArthur and became one of seven Childs locations in Canada.

Joined by several city officials and *Tribune* staff members, Mayor Webb climbed into the lead Studebaker of a twelve-car retinue at 4 a.m. and set off for Minneapolis. Their goal was a "Daylight Tour"—a trip from the heart of Winnipeg to Minneapolis city limits between dawn and dusk of a single day, around twelve hours. (A twelve-hour trip to Minneapolis may not seem so impressive today, but only a few short decades before Webb's tour, this trip would have taken a month.) This was a hard launch for Winnipeg's new Tourist Bureau and an attempt to prove that Manitoba roads weren't quite as bad as people might have heard: "Thousands of tourists from the south were halted in the vicinity of the international border last year because they were told Manitoba roads were poor. ... Such a thing cannot be allowed to happen again," proclaimed the mayor.[144]

At 4:01 p.m., just one minute behind schedule, Webb's car raced through Minneapolis city limits. By 4:24, he was banqueting with the mayor of Minneapolis. Despite a few mishaps along the way including a blown tire, a flipped car, and a broken gas line, the trip was deemed a tremendous success.[145] In the days that followed, letters flowed in to the new Tourist Bureau from curious American travellers.

The era of the car had begun at Portage and Main—but road-tripping tourists would not be enough to save Winnipeg from financial decline.

Participants in the Daylight Tour pose in front of a promotional map of their route to Minneapolis.
Winnipeg Tribune, May 16, 1925, University of Manitoba Digital Collections

Chapter 5:
The Depression

By the late 1920s the history of Portage and Main as two river trails, trodden mainly by ox carts not fifty years before, was more myth than memory. C.P. Dettloff, the *Tribune*'s chief photographer, noted with some surprise one day that the roads ran parallel to the Forks: "has it ever occurred to you that our two main thoroughfares resemble the two main rivers in many respects?"[146]

Portage and Main would have been unrecognizable to Henry McKenney. It was now the busy centre of a business district whose land value had multiplied one hundred times over since 1890.[147] The regional head office of virtually every bank in the West could be found within a block or two of the iconic Bank of Montreal Building. Lawyers, real estate agents, and insurance companies rented space in the surrounding buildings. And tucked in on Lombard, just northeast of the intersection, was the Grain Exchange: the heart of Winnipeg commerce. The activity at the Grain Exchange often "created a din that, when the windows were open, could be heard clear over to Portage and Main."[148]

The top two floors of the building were occupied by James Richardson & Sons. The company had started in Kingston, Ontario; James Richardson Sr., a tailor by trade, had allowed some customers to pay him with grain and other goods, which he found he could then sell at a profit. Soon he had set aside tailoring to become a full-time grain merchant. The company expanded westward as his sons joined in the family business. Shortly

The Grain Exchange Building, which still stands on Lombard Street
City of Winnipeg Archives

after the death of James Sr. in 1892, the company opened its first office in Winnipeg.[149]

By the late 1920s, James Richardson & Sons was firmly established in Winnipeg and its president, James Armstrong Richardson—grandson of the original James—was a proper mogul. From their offices in the Grain Exchange Building, the company expanded to radio, real estate, air travel, and oil.

But James Jr. had grander designs: a new head office that would rival any building in Winnipeg.

A Skyscraper for Winnipeg

In July 1929, the *Winnipeg Tribune* announced a new skyscraper with almost childlike glee: "Going up! Winnipeg is going up!" The new Richardson Building would be seventeen storeys and three hundred feet tall—nearly twice as tall as the next tallest office building, the Union Bank Building. It would rise fifty-eight feet above the iconic Golden Boy, and more than a hundred feet above the roof of the Fort Garry Hotel. Its location at Portage and Main signals what the intersection had become: "one of the most strategic business locations in Canada."[150]

Bylaws in Winnipeg prevented the ultra-tall skyscrapers found in other North American cities. A building could only be 1.5 times the width of the widest street it abutted and had to be set back one foot for every three feet above that limit. With Main Street measuring 132 feet wide, the top few floors of the new Richardson Building would be set back.[151]

The height of the building would be further emphasized by a giant clock tower, visible a mile away in any direction, and a revolving beacon. This huge new building would dominate Winnipeg's skyline and tower impressively over its busiest corner: "The entire aspect of Portage and Main, the central point of Great Winnipeg, will be changed."[152]

Arthur A. Stoughton, head of the school of architecture at the University of Manitoba, had been working on the plans for nearly a year. The $2-million building was to be a modern marvel, designed in a Gothic Revival style with "every feature of an up-to-date office building."[153]

Richardson was keen to see his vision come to fruition. He had spent the previous year buying up parcels of land on the northeast corner of the intersection, including the Toronto General Trusts Building and the Standard Bank Building. Excavation would begin that autumn and construction would be complete by the summer of 1930, he said.[154]

Around October 2, Richardson sent a letter to the Board of Trade indicating that construction was set to start.[155] A contract was awarded to Carter-Halls-Aldinger Ltd. As construction began and workers unearthed

Plans for a massive skyscraper to be built on the northeast corner of Portage and Main
City of Winnipeg Archives

old signs and bits of rubble, Winnipeggers became both nostalgic and optimistic: "The new Richardson sky-scraper will rise on the site which less than 50 years ago was occupied by shacks. Dimly remembered banks which have been swept away by amalgamations with their more powerful rivals have stood here, and have been succeeded by other business concerns."[156]

A wrench was soon thrown in the works. On October 24, 1929, the

Tribune announced: "Stocks and Grain Crash in Near Panic: Wall Street Values Swept Away Under Selling Avalanche."[157] The Great Depression would not be an avalanche in Manitoba, however; it would be more like a snowball—rolling downhill, slowly but surely gaining speed and mass. In fact, the next day, the *Tribune* was already reassured: "Stocks Recover; Market Chaos Ends."[158]

A crashing grain market was nothing new in Winnipeg. Though farmers resented the role of the Grain Exchange, many still bet on it. Farmers and professional traders alike made tremendous gains and then lost them all, it seemed, every few years. Perhaps the collapse, then, wasn't so out of the ordinary. As James Gray points out in his autobiographical history of the Depression *The Winter Years,* settlers to Western Canada were risktakers by nature: people who had left behind everything they knew for the promise of job or a bit of land.[159] And, he writes, they had a kind of indomitable optimism: "There has always been an ebullience about Winnipeg that the worst climate in Christendom could never suppress, a sort of what-the-hell optimism that keeps its attention permanently focused on the bright side."[160]

Winnipeg had become slowly more optimistic over the latter half of the 1920s. Recovery from the financial blows of the early 1920s was slow but steady, and the value of construction in Winnipeg had risen steadily over the past few years. Real estate companies continued to market new mansions along the riverbanks. For months, Winnipeg papers acted as if they could hold off an economic crisis simply by hoping: "Greater Winnipeg Building Prospects For Year Are Bright," they promised.[161] For Winnipeg's preeminent grain trader, however, the October crash was enough to signal what was to come.

Both the *Tribune* and the *Free Press* had run front-page features on the new Richardson tower. A much smaller piece on page four of the *Tribune* announced that work had been suspended in mid-November: "Until the business outlook in Canada shows a promise of more rapid expansion," said Richardson, "I have decided to discontinue excavation work in connection with the building we propose to erect at the corner of Portage and Main."[162] By March of the following year, the excavated site was being filled in—for safety reasons, Winnipeggers were assured.[163]

For some years, the site of the building stood empty. Mayor Webb suggested it stay this way: "This site should be purchased and the time to purchase it is now."[164] The empty lot could be beautified and become a public square or park, he suggested. Owning the lot would also allow Rorie Street to be widened, giving Winnipeg another artery more or less parallel to Main and reducing congestion.[165]

Mayor Webb lost that battle, and in 1934, the space was finally put to use for "what is claimed to be the finest service station and garage in the city of Winnipeg." The station may not have compared to the city's tallest skyscraper, but James Richardson & Sons touted its arrival nonetheless. This was to be a modern, world-class service station, both efficient

The state-of-the-art service station built on the northeast corner of Portage and Main.
Winnipeg Tribune, June 29, 1934, University of Manitoba Digital Collections

and comfortable. The customer would wait in the "tastefully decorated" lounge while their car was worked on in another wing of the building; ideally, the patron would never see an oil can.

The service station proudly proclaimed itself to be the "latest and finest link in the chain of Red Indian stations stretching across Canada," accompanied by a huge billboard featuring the profile of a man in a feathered headdress. This kind of nostalgic marketing, which harkened back to fur trade days and often used imagery of Indigenous people, is especially notable because *actual* Indigenous people had effectively been chased out of the city, confined to reserves due to the pass system.

The building itself was certainly unusual as far as service stations go. It was built in the style of an old English cottage, with timber-framed gables and "colourful beds of flowers." Contrasting this style would be the shiny, ultra-modern chromium gasoline pumps. "These pumps register the gasoline poured into the car tank by fractions of a gallon and also show the cost of the gasoline as it is pouring into the tank"—a brand-new feature at the time.[166]

This new service station, right at the heart of Winnipeg, did signal one thing aside from the declining grain market: the rise of the automobile.

Traffic Troubles

Winnipeg was, and remains, a city in want of a public square. During the Winnipeg General Strike, workers had met at Victoria Park and the Labour Temple. During the 1930s, Market Square and the grounds of the Legislative Building took over as the go-to place for politically charged speeches and discussions.

Though Winnipeg's activists had, for the time being, moved on, Portage and Main was bustling with the ordinary activities of a still growing, albeit economically troubled city:

> Winnipeg 'wakes up' at all hours of the night. If you stood at the

> corner of Portage and Main for 24 hours you would never be lonesome. [...] The pulse of the city quickens about 5 a.m. At that time the procession starts down Portage Ave., the walkers, cars and streets cars increase gradually, as first the restaurant workers, then the shop men, the early office forces, and finally the "nine-o'clockers" come to work.[167]

In 1934, *Tribune* staff photographer Claude Detloff stood at Portage and Main between 2 p.m. and 3 p.m. to count how many city-goers passed through. He counted 1,880 cars, 144 streetcars, 15 buses, 15 horse-drawn vehicles, 84 bicycles, and 4 motorcycles. Pedestrians, he said, were "too numerous to count. There were 60 to 80 persons in sight at any one moment. [...] The accumulative impression one gathers after an hour's watch is that Portage and Main is like an ant hill."[168]

Though the number of cars at Portage and Main is certainly greater today than it was in 1934, Detloff's informal survey does indicate the ways in which pedestrians and drivers were coming to terms with each other, debates which often centred on Portage and Main.

Car ownership in Manitoba had risen steadily since the early 1900s, rising to a peak of 78,850 vehicles registered in 1930. This had dwindled somewhat since the onset of the Great Depression to 68,740 in 1933. If we include only passenger cars—keeping taxi cabs in the equation but discarding tractors and ambulances and such—we find that there was one car for every 12.1 people in Manitoba.[169] For comparison, that figure today is one car per 1.6 people approximately.

Cars were not, thus, so ubiquitous as they are today. Most people who were drivers were also pedestrians, at least some of the time. But this was nevertheless a rapid change over the previous twenty-odd years, one which required pedestrians to navigate the streets in a way they had not done before, and one which required careful consideration of what space belonged to whom, and when. Did the roads belong, always, to the cars?

Moreover, with unemployment on the rise and money for leisure ac-

A car rushes through the intersection at Portage and Main
Archives of Manitoba

tivities hard to come by, it seemed that Winnipeggers had nothing better to do than stroll. People would walk down Portage, see if anything was being announced at the Free Press Building, turn at Portage and Main, and proceed down Main Street towards Market Square.[170] The result was a constant coming and going at the intersection. Those lucky enough to own cars would drive downtown in the evening, park, and then simply sit and people-watch to pass the time. "Winnipeggers were always great strollers," as James Gray put it.[171]

Walking and driving, of course, were not the only options; streetcars and buses transported many Winnipeggers into and out of the heart of the city, and Portage and Main was Winnipeg's primary transit station.

The combination of increased foot traffic and increased motor traffic made Winnipeg's streets busier and more dangerous than they had ever been before. Portage and Main, in particular, was a point of contention. Mayor Webb, who pushed tourism whenever he could, said "Every tourist that comes to Winnipeg says that Portage and Main are the most dangerous streets they have ever seen."[172]

In a 1934 letter to the editor, one reader wrote "I observe that the pedestrian is in trouble again." City council had recommended that jaywalking bylaws be strictly enforced along Portage Ave and Main St, and this particular pedestrian took umbrage. "Has the traffic committee ever enquired 'why does the pedestrian 'jay walk?'' I think not. Any one who does not own a car can answer the question. He 'jay walks' to save his life—because he is not protected when he crosses at a street corner."[173] Another letter blamed pedestrians for the state of traffic: "It does not seem fair to walk right into the traffic when a line of cars has been held up for a minute or two waiting for the green light."[174]

City Council spent much of its time debating how, and where, drivers ought to park: diagonally? Parallel? Not at all? Diagonal parking had been the norm up until now. Many argued that it ought to continue this way: that Portage and Main were both wide enough to accommodate, and that it allowed more space for shoppers to park. Of 180 downtown businesses, all but six opposed a switch to parallel parking.[175] The combination of sloppy parking and the space required for streetcar tracks, however, meant that there was often only one lane available for traffic along Portage and Main. Cars weaved in and out of the parking lane, putting pedestrians at risk. The Manitoba Motor League called the southwest corner of Portage and Main, in particular, a "dangerous bottle neck" and wrote to city council asking them to look into the problem.[176]

The debate became heated when city council voted to install "Park-O-Meters" on an experimental basis. Alderman Flye argued that motorists were already bearing too heavy a tax burden: "It was coming to the point, Ald. Flye said, where a man would be stationed at Portage and Main with a machine gun to 'pop off' motorists."

Having lost the vote, Alderman Flye declared that he would 'go down to the legislature and oppose this thing.' 'That's all right,' said Ald. Blumberg. 'Somehow I think you'd be better off down there.' 'Would they be better off?' smiled Ald. Honeyman."[177]

Pedestrian injuries were relatively frequent at Portage and Main (albeit less common than in the North End, where Winnipeg police bemoaned that drivers needed to pay more attention). In 1933 an eighty-year-old man was hit by a car, fortunately escaping with only minor injuries.[178] Another forty-year-old man collided with a car while riding his bike.[179]

One young man even managed to be hit by both a streetcar *and* an automobile: crossing against the light he dashed past the front of the streetcar and into the path of the automobile, which struck him and threw him *back* into the path of the streetcar, which then also hit him. The man "was found lying beside the front exit of the street car" and was dazed but seemed otherwise okay after being taken to the hospital.[180]

Even wildlife was not spared: one Hungarian partridge had to be taken home by the electric traffic supervisor at Portage and Main after being hit by a streetcar. The bird eventually recovered and was released at the limits of West Kildonan, eagerly flying away from the city.[181]

A five-part series in the *Tribune* coinciding with the Board of Trade's nine-day Safe Driving Contest investigated the causes and possible solutions to Winnipeg's traffic problems: in 1937, 31 people had been killed and 562 injured across the city.[182] The problem stemmed from both the pedestrian and driver sides of the equation, the series concluded.

"What can be done about the pedestrians?" asked the *Tribune*. "There are

A man stands at Portage and Main as cars and streetcars rush through behind him.
Archives of Manitoba

few cities where jay-walking is so reckless and so accepted a habit as in this city."[183] Part of the problem were the streets themselves: Portage and Main were both so wide that getting across on a green light could be challenging for any pedestrian who did not catch the light as soon as it changed. Pedestrians frequently found themselves, through no real fault of their own, in the middle of the road when the light changed to red. Instead, they got into the habit of simply dashing across wherever and whenever they saw a gap in traffic.

Drivers were also a problem: 80% of accidents happened "on dry roads in clear weather," implying that they were avoidable. Some 10% were due to drunk driving. "The greatest number of drivers who have accidents are neither physically defective nor ignorant of traffic rules. They take chances by going to fast; they pass other cars on hills and curves or on the right; they do not slow down or stop at intersection; they expect other drivers and pedestrians to get out of their way regardless of traffic conditions."[184] The most hazardous habit of drivers was to blindly turn right on a red light, forcing pedestrians to scurry back to the sidewalk.

City Council seemed hesitant to make real changes to regulate traffic, however. They banned right turns on red lights altogether and then rolled this back. Jaywalking was prohibited, then later simply "frowned upon." They hoped that the parade of drivers from the Safe Driving Contest could set an example: "Driving in the parade, they will not only demonstrate how to drive a car safely, courteously and well, but will be perfect examples of the truism that safe driving does pay."[185]

Both pedestrians and drivers accepted new regulations only begrudgingly, in any case. Portage and Main had been one of the first intersections in the city to get a traffic signal (an "American Bobby"-style signal which sat at the centre of the intersection), supplementing and eventually replacing the police officer controlling the intersection. Eventually modern four-corner-style traffic lights were placed at twenty intersections along Portage Avenue and Main Street.[186] Several letters to the editor pronounced the perceived foolishness of putting traffic lights at *every* intersection: "Autos are not so thick in Winnipeg that it is necessary to have signals at all corners"[187]

Attempts to regulate jaywalking met similar resistance: "The old notion of the street as the king's highway on which the pedestrian may claim a prior right dies hard. ... For better or for worse motor vehicle traffic, dense and dangerous, is here to stay."[188]

The Place to Be

Aside from James A. Richardson's scrapped skyscraper and the new service station built in its place, the corners of Portage and Main saw few architectural changes during the Great Depression—a symptom, perhaps, of the lack of investment during this period. One letter-writer even suggested that the city offer free vacant land within one mile of Portage and Main to anyone who promised to build on it in a sort of urban homesteading scheme.[189] A few federally funded projects did materialize nearby; notably, the Federal Building at 269 Main Street was built in 1936 as an unemployment relief project. It replaced the previous Industrial Bureau Exposition Building, which had stood for less than twenty-five years.

Portage and Main was often the focus of civic efforts towards modernizing and beautifying the city, however. In late 1929, despite the encroaching economic downturn, the Board of Trade promised that this December would be "the gayest Christmas the historic thoroughfare has

Portage and Main decorated for Christmas in 1929. An early traffic light can be seen on the right.
Martin Berman Collection, Winnipeg Public Library

ever known." Lights were strung across Portage and Main, and merchants at the intersection collaborated with the board to set up decorations, with some three hundred trees mounted on lampposts. Their bright colours would "transform [Portage and Main], when the current is switched on tonight, into a Yuletide fairyland." The following year the ongoing drought nearly cancelled the decorations due to Winnipeg's reliance on hydroelectric power, but the Christmas spirit (and increased water flow) ultimately prevailed.[190]

The lights across Portage and Main were lit again for the King's Jubilee, and for a bicentenary celebration of the arrival of La Verendrye to Red River.[191] At Easter, a fifty-pound chocolate Easter egg appeared at the corner, courtesy of Bond & Ronald Ltd—today called Cavalier Candies.[192]

Proximity to Portage and Main was highly desirable. Fully half of Winnipeg's approximately 280,000 residents lived within a mile and a half of the intersection, and it seemed that this was where they wanted to stay.[193] Businesses and real estate were advertised according to their proximity: a pharmacy was "6 Minutes Walk to Portage and Main;" an apartment for rent was "15 mins. walk to cor. Portage and Main."[194] Even seventy acres of farmland were advertised as being "5 miles from Portage and Main."[195]

As Winnipeg's busiest corner, this was also where those collecting for charity tended to go. "Tag days," charity sales of paper tags worn on one's lapel, were common throughout this period. "My hands are cold, but I'm selling my poppies," said a young woman selling tags for Remembrance Day from Winnipeg's windiest corner.[196] Thirteen years in a row, "Vic" sold tags at Portage and Main for the Humane Society—along with his human, Mrs. J. Webb.[197] (Mrs. Webb moved her collecting to Portage and Donald after Vic passed away in 1937.) Even the unemployed tried their hand at a tag day, though with little success.

The corner did see an increase in petty crime during this period, likely due to the economic downturn. One Humane Society tagger faced off with a "big, red-faced man" who attempted, unsuccessfully, to take her collections box.[198] In 1936, a panhandler named James Allen Gould was

Vic the Dog, who collected money for the Humane Society at Portage and Main
Winnipeg Tribune, June 12, 1931, University of Manitoba Digital Collections

given twenty-four hours to leave town after "grabbing a citizen by the arm and asking for a dollar."

Nevertheless, Portage and Main was a convenient meeting place: for snowshoeing clubs, hiking clubs, golfing clubs and so on, it sufficed to print a quick ad in the papers noting a date and time to meet at Portage and Main. Then, since it was a busy streetcar stop, members could easily proceed to wherever their destination happened to be.

Winnipeg's love for a good parade continued through the 1930s despite the economic downturn—perhaps even because of it. In October of

1930, "Canadian Prosperity Week" was capped off by a lengthy parade that would take paraders down Main Street, turning at Portage and Main, down Portage then onto Osborne, Corydon, down Stafford, and finally over the Maryland bridge back to Portage Ave. This was to be "a demonstration sponsored by the theatres of Canada and participated in by Canadian business men to dispel gloom and restore confidence and goodwill to the Dominion."[199]

The route of this parade was a bit of an exception; most parades began somewhere around City Hall, turned at Portage and Main, and then continued west down Portage—or sometimes vice-versa. The parades that passed through our iconic intersection tell us something about what was important to Winnipeg at the time. Each year, a grand Decoration Day parade would pay tribute to the men who fought in the First World War. In 1937, members of seventeen Orange Lodges and members of nine women's lodges marched down Portage and Main towards Knox Church. Another parade that year advertised an upcoming horse show.

And, of course, there were the unemployed.

Unemployed Protests

As unemployment ramped up through the 1930s, reaching its height towards the end of the decade, single unemployed men formed associations protesting not only their unemployment but the quality of relief: the quality of food at soup kitchens, the cleanliness of the plates and cutlery, the state of available housing, and more. Unemployed marches took place in virtually every city across Canada, with Winnipeg being no exception.

The 1930s were also a time of radical politics. The system that had been established, many felt, was broken. Perhaps it felt even more so in Winnipeg, where the troubled economy of the early 1920s had seen barely five years of recovery before the subsequent crash. Those who were most affected looked for ways to change the system.

Winnipeg communists and anarchists saw more success during any other

An unemployed march upon the Legislative Building in 1931
Archives of Manitoba

period before or since. Among a handful of socialists elected to city office, Jacob Penner is perhaps the most notable. Penner was a popular North End alderman who was elected in 1934 and held his seat until 1961, the only gap being the two years during which he was interned as a "known and dangerous communist" during World War Two.[200]

In 1930, Penner and several other local communist leaders gave speeches at Market Square. Nearly a thousand men and women were in attendance. As they marched south led by Alderman Kolisnyk—the first Communist ever elected to office in North America—they were stopped at Portage and Main. Police seized the large banner they were carrying: "1914 Heroes –1930 Vagrants." Bannerless, they were allowed to continue their march to the Legislative Building where they presented a list of demands to Premier Bracken. On the legislative grounds a fight broke out between the unemployed communists and a large group of university students. The students sang "O Canada" while the marchers sang "The Internationale," both trying to drown out the other group and finally coming to blows. Eventually both groups were separated and dispersed by the provincial police.[201]

The summer of 1936 was deadly hot. This was the era of the Dust Bowl, and this was the worst of it. Temperatures reached above 42 degrees Celsius (hotter, according to unofficial readings) on the weekend of July 12, but this did not keep protesters home. If anything, the heat and the worsening unemployment rate combined to heighten tensions. There was a "brush" that Sunday night between the police and a group of unemployed men at Portage and Main. Led by Alderman Penner, a crowd had marched from Memorial Boulevard to Portage and Main, where "there was a slight outbreak of disorder." Some of the marchers walked in the street, and one pulled a streetcar trolley off the wire. Three policemen were injured trying to force the marchers back onto the sidewalks.[202]

At a city council meeting, Alderman Penner insisted that the matter be investigated. Mayor John Queen pushed back that the men had been carrying baseball bats, instigating the fight.[203] But the matter was relegated to page five of the *Tribune*, for good reason: twenty-two people had died that weekend from the heat, and eight more had drowned trying to cool off in the rivers.[204]

This particular scuffle was part of an ongoing series of protests that

Rupert Avenue police station, where unemployed protesters were jailed for failing to pay streetcar fares

City of Winnipeg Archives

had begun that spring. In May, three hundred members of the Single Men's Unemployed Association had marched single file down the sidewalks of Portage and Main with signs asking for better conditions for those on relief: "Citizens' enquiry committee condemns soup kitchens;" "We want doctors of our own choice;" "Unite in this campaign." Premier Bracken refused to meet with their delegation, but the marchers were allowed to complete their protest—followed but unbothered by police officers—and return to their hall at 217 Logan Ave.[205]

Things got more serious in June. One evening, thirty-eight men boarded a streetcar at Portage and Main. They walked silently past the conductor and sat down, refusing to pay their fares when pressed. Another twenty or so boarded another streetcar at Main and Higgins. Police were notified and both cars were stopped at Main and Rupert, near the police station. The men on the second streetcar were let off with a warning, while all thirty-eight from the Portage and Main car were arrested.

On June 24, several hundred of the single unemployed marched down Main Street to the Rupert Street Police Station where they sang and shouted to the men in jail before police forced them to leave. The men were charged and then released three at a time, crossing the street to join their cheering companions.[206]

Alderman Forkin—another of Winnipeg's communists—said: "The system of mass feeding, house and clothing is demoralizing." The *Tribune* accused Forkin of exaggerating when he also called the system "degrading and inhuman," but Forkin had captured precisely the discontent of the unemployed.[207] It was bad enough to be out of work, but the system of relief that kept men alive was often humiliating, forcing men into crowded and dirty dining halls and unpleasant housing situations. Some advocated for restaurant and hotel vouchers that would allow unemployed men to make their own choices on these matters.

A committee studying the problem suggested some minor changes: additional space for dining halls, better dishes and cutlery, and occasional changes to the menu. The protests continued, though with some difficulty.[208] Winnipeg did not have, after all, a public square. The July protest at Portage and Main—the one that ended in a scuffle with police—had first been planned for the Legislative grounds, but Jacob Penner was told that this would be viewed as trespassing and that they would be removed with force, "if necessary."

In mid-July, several of the thirty-eight streetcar protesters went to trial. While a crowd protested across from the police station, sixteen men were convicted of refusing to pay their fare and given a choice of a $5 fine or seven days in jail. Six more were convicted of "parading without a permit" and given either $10 fine or ten days in jail. All twenty-two men took the jail term. Four more men would face charges relating to "being members of an unlawful assembly," and might face riot charges. Douglas Grainger, convicted of refusing to pay his fare, told the court "they had been found guilty of trying to improve their conditions of life. 'I'll go out and do the same thing over and over again.'"[209]

Portage and Main was still welcome to most Winnipeggers in the 1930s: to clubs, to commuters, and even to the occasional parade. Bankers, lawyers, and real estate agents were most certainly welcome. It is worth considering, however, who was not made welcome. Winnipeg had firmly established that Portage and Main, after 1919, was not a place for agitators and activists. A person could quietly press their cause at the intersection by selling tags or handing out pamphlets. But Communists and the angry unemployed were to take their business elsewhere—or ideally, nowhere at all.

Chapter 6

Portage and Main Takes Centre Stage

For much of the early twentieth century, Winnipeg's Market Square was a major gathering place. Tucked away behind city hall and bustling with commerce, this was where all manner of parades and protests were held. It was closed in 1919 following the Winnipeg General Strike and turned into civic offices, and while it was used sporadically as a public gathering spot, Winnipeg lacked a true public square. This meant that when the Second World War began, there was no obvious space for rallies and demonstrations sparked by Canada's involvement in it. A number of spaces across the city were utilized, including indoors at the Civic Auditorium and outside on the grounds of the Legislature, but Portage and Main was due to play a role in the fundraising efforts to come.

The Battle at Portage and Main

A major fundraising effort put forward by the Canadian government were Victory Loan drives. These loans, also called War Bonds, were a method for the government to fundraise for the war effort without drastically raising taxes. Businesses and members of the public were encouraged to do their civic duty and purchase bonds, with the hope of returns once the war had ended.

Advertisements for the sale of Victory Loans were a common sight in the newspaper, but larger initiatives were needed to spur the public into action. From this idea came War Loan and Victory Loan Drives, nation-wide fundraising campaigns. Each province had its own fundraising body, made up of local businessmen, salesmen, and politicians who could come up with unique programming to support the war effort. Goals were set by province and by city across each of the drives, and on the whole Canadians exceeded these financial goals every time.

There were two National War Bond Drives in Canada, followed by nine Victory Loan Drives spanning from 1940 to 1945. Each incorporated patriotic concerts, displays, and contests in Winnipeg—coupled with some larger scale publicity events. The second war bond drive, in February of 1941, saw Winnipeg's first effort at a large-scale publicity event.

'The Battle at Portage and Main' took place at noon on February 7, the first day of the war savings drive. Following a warning alert from the *Free Press's* emergency siren at 11:45 a.m., people rushed from their offices to crowd around Portage and Main. For the interested crowd, an officer narrated the events over a loudspeaker. Members of the 13th Field Regiment, Royal Canadian Artillery held the crowds back as motorcycles reached the intersection. Field guns soon followed, as soldiers dismounted their motorcycles and took position behind anti-tank guns positioned strategically on the north and west corners.

Then there was someone yelling "Gas!", and "The men in the street became ghouls—strange, fierce-looking men of another world—as they put their masks on."[210] The crowd, which had turned quiet and tense over the course of the twenty-minute display, appeared suitably affected. "Thank heavens this is only in fun," a *Free Press* reporter recalled someone saying.[211]

The whole thing was over in less than an hour, but it set the tone for the events to come. The following year, for an eight-day drive scheduled for June, Portage and Main was the hub of operations. An eighteen-pound cannon was placed outside of the Bank of Montreal, alongside a giant thermometer with airplane markers. Each day at noon, the cannon would fire off: one shot for each million raised. And for those passing through downtown at any other hour, a simple glance at the thermometer would show much was raised. The first day of the campaign was promising: the cannon was fired three times, signaling three million raised before the day was even done! Premier Stuart Garson was present to give opening remarks, as were a contingent of buglers and military regiments.[212]

The schedule of events included concerts, parades, a bicycle decorating contest, poster decorating, and a series of bonfires led by the Boy Scouts. The highlight of the drive was set for Wednesday, June 4, right in the middle of the campaign. It promised something Winnipeg had never seen before and hopefully never would again: a blackout.

Major H.S. Hanson, the chairman of the Blackout Committee, had organized a true spectacle for the evening. In an interview, Hansom promised: "all the bedlam and fury of total war will be loosed on the heart of the city. It will be like London, Rotterdam or Belgrade at their worst—without the bloodshed."[213] The event was meant to replicate the conditions experienced across European cities, where blackouts were enforced to keep the city in total darkness to protect from targeted aerial attacks.

Following a 9:55 p.m. alert siren, all lights within the defined boundaries were to be turned off. Drivers were instructed to pull over and shut off their headlights, and pedestrians were reminded to stay on the sidewalk and avoid smoking. More than 75,000 people flocked downtown, crowding around major intersections, to watch the evening proceed.[214]

Radio station CKY had a live broadcast of the demonstration, with reporters stationed at four locations in the blackout zone. CKY reporter Wilf Davidson had a prime view from the Winnipeg's tallest building, the thirteen-storey Childs building at the northwest corner of Portage and Main.[215] *Tribune* writer Vic Murray and his wife, actress Jean Kirk, had a view from the ground outside of the CKY office on Portage and Main—where in the pitch blackness, neither realized they were standing next to an anti-aircraft gun (an 'ack ack') until it went off next to them. [216]

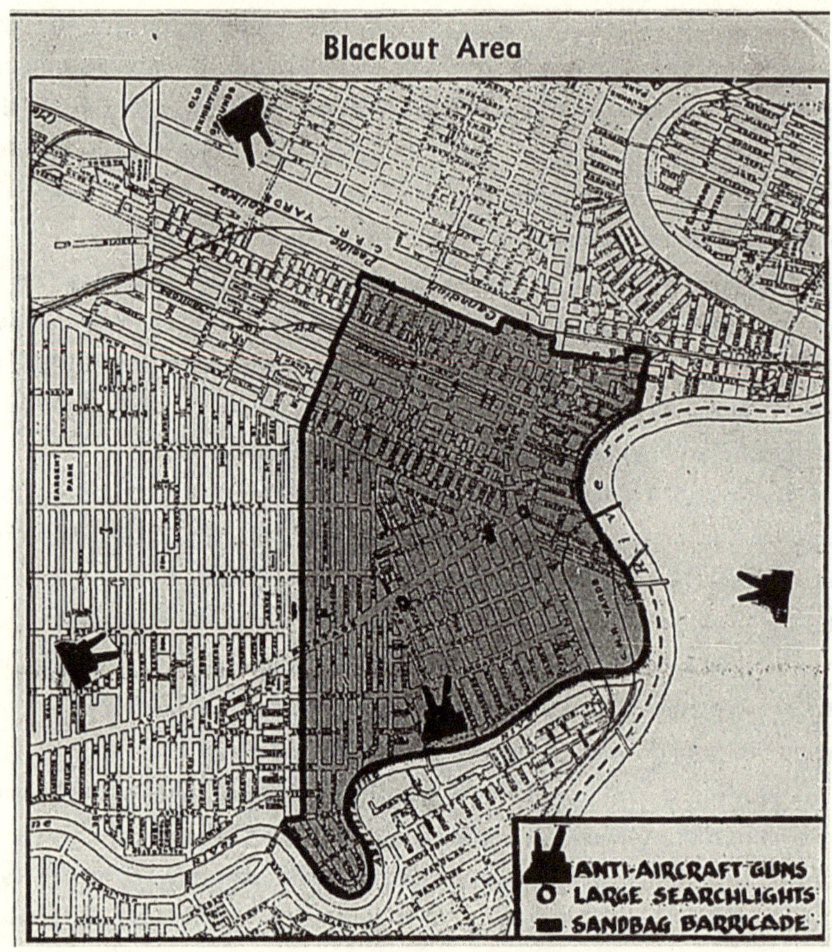

A map depicting the blackout event boundaries
Winnipeg Evening Tribune, June 4, 1941 Winnipeg Tribune Archives/University of Manitoba

Searchlights swept the sky for any sign of 'enemy' aircraft, and airplanes whirred noisily overhead. Mock battles were fought along Portage Avenue. For Davidson, standing at the top of Childs Building, none of this was visible. Winnipeg was hidden under "clouds of sulphuric smoke, swept up into the night and into the streets below."[217] Bursts of light came from neighbouring rooftops, as members of the Winnipeg Skeet Club and Winnipeg Gun Club fired shotguns into the sky.

The lights flickered back on at 10:30 p.m., the smell of smoke lingering in the air. Children played atop the sandbag barricades and, ignoring the uptick in victory loan donations, it was as if Winnipeg had never been bombed at all.

Subsequent drives also set up outside of the Bank of Montreal, which by 1943 was dubbed Victory Square. The exact layout depended on the drive, but for each one there was a Victory Loan Tower (a raised platform to give speeches), and the cannon and large map that become a staple of these events. For one drive, a large map of Germany was mounted and for each amount of money raised sections of the map were marked off.

The most remembered of these Victory Loan drives is 1942's If Day, a mock-Nazi invasion of Winnipeg that saw a swastika hung above city, the *Winnipeg Tribune* renamed and printed in badly translated German, and city officials arrested. It was the most substantial of the Victory Loan Drives. Winnipeg was aiming to raise $23,569,000 for the drive, Manitoba a whopping $45 million. Many of the activities were focused on Winnipeg's business district. Volunteers, dressed in rented Nazi costumes from Hollywood, raided the Great West Life building, accosted pedestrians on streetcars and roamed Winnipeg's streets. During the morning's mock battle, 'Nazi' troops rode down Portage Avenue with Bren gun carriers.

Unlike the previous war demonstrations which only lasted about half an hour, If Day lasted from seven in the morning until 5:30 in the evening. Participants in the event ended the day with a parade down Portage Avenue, culminating at Portage and Main. A forty-foot map of Manitoba was hung outside of the Bank of Montreal, divided into forty-five sections—one for each of the million dollars Manitoba aimed to raise. For each million dollars, a union jack sticker would be placed on a section of the map to "symbolize the 'reoccupation' of the province following IF DAY."[218] Nearly $15 million was raised by the end of If Day, and at the end of drive on March 9, Manitoba had raised $65 million. The map at Portage and Main was covered in Union Jacks. Manitoba had been liberated.

(above) The Victory Loan Tower ceremony at Portage and Main, May 30, 1945
Foote 2361, L.B. Foote Collection, Archives of Manitoba

(below) The Victory Loan Tower, looking south down Main Street. May 12, 1945
Foote 2362, L.B. Foote Collection, Archives of Manitoba

As the war drew on, fundraising drives began to include materials needed for the war effort. Public events were held across 1943 to encourage the public to donate whatever good fit the theme of the month. March was fats, April rags, and June and July saw asks for metals.

To promote the summer metal drive, another map was placed at Portage and Main: Germany, this time, not Manitoba, with an allied bomber flying overhead. As metal donations came in, German cities were 'bombed' off the map. The text on the sign read: 'Your scrap metal will blast and break 'em.'[219]

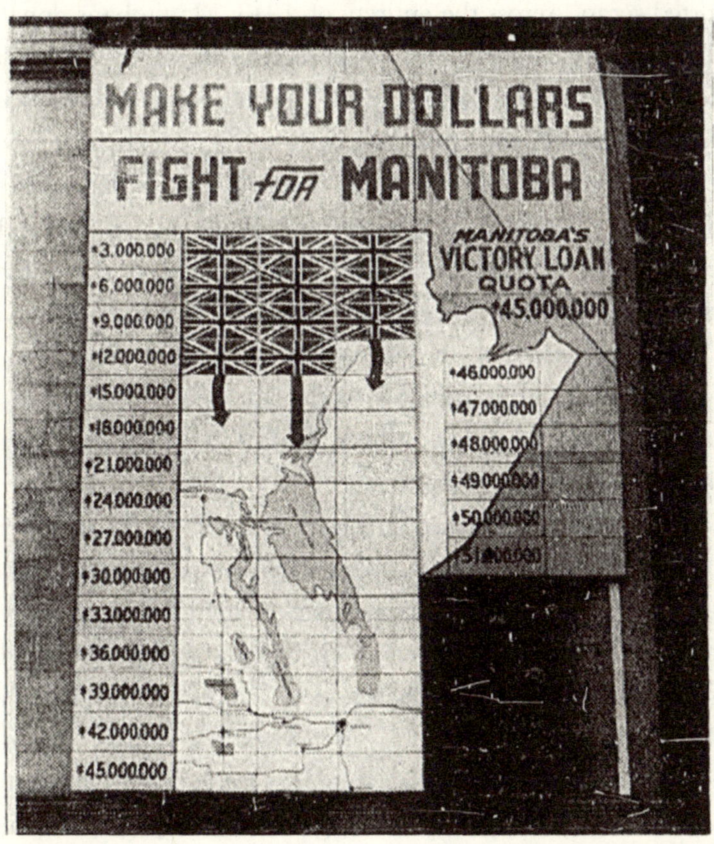

A Map of Manitoba hung on the Bank of Montreal.
Winnipeg Evening Tribune, February 20, 1942 Winnipeg Tribune Archives/ University of Manitoba

For the opening parade, hundreds of Winnipeg children marched from Memorial Boulevard down Portage Avenue to the Bank of Montreal, pulling decorated wagons filled with scrap metals. Brass bands, stationed along the street, played marching tunes for the passing children.

Mayor George Garnet Coulter of Winnipeg and Mayor George MacLean of St. Boniface were waiting at Portage and Main, with other political officials—as were army trucks to haul the scrap metal away. The whole thing was broadcast on radio stations CKY and CJRC. The Patriotic Salvage Corp, the organizers for the drive, were looking to bring in 2,000 tons of assorted scrap. Across the entirety of 1943, Manitobans donated over 94 million pounds of scrap and established thrift stores to sell additional donations found with the salvage. Enid V. Nemy, with the Canadian Press, observed that "Manitobans collect more than twice as much salvage as does the average Canadian."[220] Our penchant for holding on to things had paid off.

Given the importance the intersection had taken on in war fundraising, it was natural that when an armistice was announced on May 7, thousands rushed to the intersection to celebrate, despite lingering snow and a biting wind. Pedestrians crowded the sidewalk around the Victory Loan Tower, jostling each other and darting across the slow-moving stream of cars on the roads. Drivers, in cars packed like sardine cans, honked and shouted out into the general din on the street.

Air force officers, standing on top of the Victory Loan tower, threw confetti onto the street below. Another man on the street, finding himself without confetti, ticker tape, or streamers, settled for grabbing a bag of seeds and sending that into the wind. "If wheat starts growing on the city's main streets," the *Winnipeg Tribune* quipped, "credit will be due to this modern Johnny Appleseed who did his Victory seeding today."[221]

Inspired by the Victory Loan campaigns during war time, Portage and Main continued to serve as a fundraising site in Winnipeg during the 1950s. This time, the goal was philanthropic, through Community Chest Campaigns. Now known as the United Way, community chest drives had been organized in Winnipeg since 1923 to raise funds for social causes. From

V-Day at Portage and Main as seen from the Victory Loan Tower
Winnipeg Tribune May 7, 1945 Winnipeg Tribune Archives/University of Manitoba

1956-1961, Portage and Main became a focal point for the drive—with a large thermometer placed at the intersection to display how much money had been raised (with the exception being that, in 1959, a large cash register was placed at the intersection instead). One advertisement, boasting that the campaign had raised over 60% of the funds needed for the fundraising drive, also highlighted the growing concerns about traffic in Winnipeg. "Your contribution to the Community Chest is a direct investment in the future of a child who needs help," Constable Ted Ryland of the School Patrol wrote in a publicity brief. "You wouldn't run him down on the street; neither will you let him down when he is depending on you."[222]

The Community Chest Thermometer at Portage and Main, Oct 12, 1957
Winnipeg Tribune Photo Collection, University of Manitoba Archives

Winnipeg Turns 75

Though Winnipeg's actual incorporation date would not come around until fall, the city opted to host their celebrations in the first week of June in 1949, when the weather was warmer and the day longer. It was a week-long party, with plans spanning across the city. There were public works projects, a new fountain on Memorial at St. Mary's, and two hundred lampposts with technicolour bulbs were spread across Portage Avenue and Main Street. Planning the event was a substantial effort, with sixty-one birthday committees and 260 organizations involved. George Waight, a Winnipeg performer, would coordinate twenty-two shows for the week.

The showstopper was at Portage and Main. A 64-foot-high cake sculpture, which consisted of "a white cake base 30 feet in diameter supporting 45-foot high red and white numeral "75", which will be outlined at night in neon lights. There will also be 75 lighted candles around the top of the cake." Each day, there would be a cake ceremony set on a viewing platform at the intersection—and, on each day, there was a theme with specific events and ceremonies:

Winnipeg's 75th Birthday Cake
William Kenyon, Miscellaneous Collection [A0163-5115], University of Winnipeg Archives

Sunday, June 5: Commemoration and Decoration Day
Monday, June 6: Civic and Farmers Day.
Tuesday, June 7: Canada Day
Wednesday, June 8: American Day.
Thursday, June 9: United Citizens Day
Friday, June 10: British Commonwealth Day
Saturday, June 11: Winnipeg Day

Cake ceremonies would take place at noon, and the scheduled event depended on the theme of the day. On Civic and Farmers day, Mayor Garnet Coulter had organized a display called "Operation Mayor." For the thousands gathered at the intersection, the first announcement they heard was "five miles southeast of Headingley, cruising at 375 miles per hour." Then, there was the shriek of aircraft as two Vampfire fighters whooshed overhead, just clearing the Childs building on the corner. A performance followed on the viewing platform.

There was a guest of honour at the festivities: Alexis Smith. Smith, an actress and singer, was born in British Columbia before moving to Los Angeles and entering showbiz. By 1949, she had starred alongside Jack Benny, Errol Flynn, Ronald Reagan, and Humphrey Bogart (alongside many others) and had come to Winnipeg as the guest of honour for the festival. Smith, alongside her husband Craig Stevens (best known as the star of the TV series *Peter Gunn*), spent the week in Winnipeg and took part in a variety of the festivities. On June 8, for American Day (which happened to be Smith's birthday), the crowd gathered at Portage and Main to sing happy birthday to the actress.

There was a large influx of tourists from across the province and the United States coming in for the festivities. A pair of siblings, former Winnipeggers Ken and Grace Todd, rented a plane to fly in from their home in Los Angeles. Ken flew the plane, a single-engine Beechcraft, while his sister navigated. Another man flew in from Smith River, California, making a detour from the 52-aircraft tour group he was travelling with. Locals saw relatives from Ireland and England. With this rise in tourism came rises in concern about petty theft. The constant clusters of people around areas like Portage and Main meant lots of easy targets for "Dips" or pickpockets. *Tribune* reporter Harold Miloff had spent nearly every day that week out on the streets, observing pickpockets to record their tricks and provide tips to the general public. Ironically, Miloff himself was pickpocketed, and his notes were stolen.

The final day of the festival, Winnipeg Day, saw a lunch at Assiniboine Park, archery exhibitions and bike races, a "Wild Wind-up" for teenagers, an ice carnival with Canadian figure skater Barbara Ann Scott, and a midnight closing ceremony at Portage and Main. Around 5,000 people were gathered to watch the candles be "blown out" just after midnight.

Off the Rails

Despite the fact that Portage and Main had been a meeting place throughout the war years, traffic policies, on the whole, were becoming increasingly anti-pedestrian in the postwar era.

The difficulties with jaywalking that had plagued the 1930s had not improved, despite the introduction of pedestrian crossing signals in 1950. Scramble crossings were also suggested, at least by one *Winnipeg Tribune* reader, who wrote the paper to ask about its feasibility. W.H. Finnbogason, Winnipeg's traffic engineer, replied that "Portage and Main [were] both too wide for scrambles. Average walker would take 40 seconds to cross either one diagonally. An extra stop of that length would impede vehicular flow almost to blockage point."[223]

A massive traffic by-law amendment in 1951 finally did what Winnipeg had tried to do twenty years earlier: jaywalking was now illegal. The same amendments also gave pedestrians the right of way when cars were making left or right turns and stipulated that motorists must not "cut in or weave through traffic" and must stop at all stop signs, among other rules. Jaywalking was the main talking point, regardless of the other rules introduced. Shortly before the new traffic by-law took effect, an anonymous writer under the name Nimble Foot, penned the "Jaywalkers Lament" to the *Winnipeg Tribune*:

> As the deadline of May 12 approaches, it may not be inopportune to shed a tear for the plight of the Winnipeg pedestrian. On this date he says goodbye to his cherished freedom to risk life and limb in random

> crossings of his city's streets. Almost it seems as if the end of an era were at hand. No longer will he be able to dodge to safety islands in the face of vehicular traffic, no longer defy the onrushing auto or the lumbering bus. The symptoms of modernity, in the form of traffic controls, have caught up with him.[224]

Campaigns against "Winnipeg's favourite sport" continued through the 1950s, ranging from stationed police constables blowing whistles at passing jaywalkers to $1-2 fines to anyone caught crossing the street illegally.[225] Despite the crackdowns, jaywalking near Portage and Main remained a problem—in part because pedestrians were taking refuge at the safety islands dotted across the thoroughfares. The safety islands were in place to accommodate transit riders, as the streetcar tracks ran down the middle of the roads.

For Winnipeg's public transit network, Portage and Main was a major transfer hub. Thousands of Winnipeggers were funneled through that intersection every day at all hours, from 5:30 a.m. to 1:38 a.m. the following morning. Public transit ridership in Winnipeg reached an all-time high in 1946, with 105,000,000 passengers annually.[226]

The streetcar system, however, was old and expensive to maintain and took up considerable space on the road. Car ownership had increased dramatically over the 1950s, jumping from 65,511 in 1953 to 92,000 in 1957. This increase in cars led to an increasing demand for road and parking space. And the streetcars, clunky and outdated with tracks taking up major road space, were in the way.

Alternative options were already being used by the city. Winnipeg had used gasoline-powered buses since 1918 for feeder routes in other neighbourhoods, and the city had started using trolley buses in lieu of streetcars by 1938. While these buses still relied on the same overhead wires as the streetcar for power, they did not need tracks and were a cheaper and more flexible option for the city. As a result, streetcars were slowly phased out and replaced by the trolley buses—until, in 1955, Winnipeg discontinued streetcar use for good.[227]

Opinions on the matter were mixed. Some were nostalgic, others excited about the prospect of modernization. Regardless, on September 19, 1955, thousands gathered at Portage and Main for the final day of streetcar service. A farewell procession had been planned as four streetcars rode south down Main Street. All were occupied by city and transit officials. First to go was a wooden streetcar from 1909, followed by a 1918 sweeper truck that had been used clear the lines, and finally two steel cars built in the 1920s. With a painted tear rolling down the side of the front window, Winnipeg's last streetcar made a farewell voyage down Main Street. Mayor George Sharpe, alongside twelve reeves, were gathered at Portage and Main to perform an unusual task: to symbolically sever the transit line by removing a small portion of the track.

Portage Avenue looking west towards Main Street with visible traffic islands
City of Winnipeg Archives, 1940

Winnipeg's last streetcar ride
Archives of Manitoba

The concrete safety islands, which were bulky and took up valuable road space, were slowly removed, and the remaining streetcar tracks were slated to be pulled up in the coming years. There was now significantly more space at Portage and Main, and traffic engineers began coming up with new concepts for the intersection, both practical and otherwise.

One 1956 proposal was the introduction of a twenty-four-foot freeway at Portage and Main for transit and emergency service vehicles, another involved centre street parking. Both ideas were rejected by the Winnipeg traffic commission, who instead proposed to install a ten-foot boulevard with grass and small trees to beautify the area and control traffic. This idea proved divisive, literally, in council. Alderman Frank Wagner opposed the proposed width, suggesting that "if there is to be a divider, it should be of solid concrete and not more than four feet wide."[228]

Public opinion leaned in favour of boulevards. When interviewed, local union leaders all expressed variations on the sentiment. Harvey Barber of the Autoworkers Union wrote: "Make this a prairie garden city, with parking lots of back streets and a lawn strip down Portage Avenue."

An artistic rendering of a monorail running through Portage and Main
Winnipeg Evening Tribune, January 11, 1962, Winnipeg Tribune Archives/University of Manitoba

Chris Schubert, of the Retail Wholesale and Department Store Union, considered pedestrian safety, saying that they "must have some space to halt upon while crossing if necessary—a green strip would be the answer."[229]

There were detractors. Gordon Ritchie, also with the Retail Wholesale and Department Store Union, believed that a new boulevard would increase congestion. Support from Mayor George Sharpe and public works pushed the project forward despite the opposition.

More novel ideas came in the following years. A Toronto civil engineer, Norman Wilson, proposed subway lines in 1959—this was scrapped due to high costs and a fear that water from the Red and Assiniboine Rivers would seep in. The Winnipeg Metro Transit director, D.I. McDonald, proposed a monorailinWinnipegin1962.InspiredbytheWorld'sFairmonorailinSeattle, McDonald envisioned parallel monorail lines running along major thoroughfares. It would, he admitted, be ugly and he was unsure how Winnipeg's climate would impact operations. Neither of these options went further than the ideas stage, but the monorail captured the imagination of Stephen Juba. It remained a passion project for Juba for much of his time as mayor.

The University of Portage and Main

Every October, from the 1930s until the early 1970s, there was one consistent event that broke the monotony of downtown's every day traffic: The University of Manitoba's annual "Freshie" Parade.

Held in October as part of the University's Freshman Week, the parade was a chance to welcome new arrivals and highlight the creativity of the school's varied faculty. The tradition began in 1937, under the leadership of University of Manitoba Student Union President Ron Howard. These parades would continue until 1971, with an eight-year gap from 1939-1945 during World War Two. Though the parade route varied slightly over the years, it always involved passing through Portage and Main.

Howard led the way for the inaugural parade, riding a white horse. He confided in a reporter for *The Manitoban*, though, that he had been cautioned about his mount. "I had been warned by the milk company from which the horse was borrowed that it had never been ridden before and might at any moment get a longing for its milk route and start off towards Norwood."[230]

Another section of *The Manitoban* quipped: "When interviewed after the parade, Mr. Turner's horse was non-committal. Did he think the parade was a good thing? Nay. Was his master kind of him? He refused to be quoted."[231]

By the 1940s, the parades had become more automobile heavy. The 1946 parade featured just thirteen horses, but six tractors, one ambulance, two beer wagons, three motorcycles, twenty-five cars, and an "atomic cow." Tragically, no photos exist of the futurist bovine—part of a float that advertised ice cream for the Faculty of Agriculture.

Most departments spent time creating unique floats, with some kind of gag, gimmick, or performance. The law school's float featured a full courtroom, with a female judge overseeing the proceedings (unusual for 1946—the first female judge in Canada had just been appointed in 1943). A sheriff, running alongside the float, 'subpoenaed' members of the crowd and hustled them to the float to face trial. The Department of Agriculture had *five* floats, including the aforementioned atomic cow, and another featuring a barn dance.

This was an annual staple, and a best float was selected by a jury each year. Usually, this jury was made up of university faculty, peers, or community members, but in 1949 the students were treated to special celebrity guest: Nat King Cole.

The American jazz singer sat at a judging table at Portage Avenue and Donald Street as the procession passed by. The floats were theatrical; the law school was back with their mock-court, the Department of Architecture had built a shaking log cabin, and science students had built a rocket from Mars. Cole, interviewed in the *Free Press*, said the event was "imaginative" and "enthusiastic," and awarded the Department of Home Economics best float. It featured six women, dressed in formal white gowns, holding orchids.[232]

Freshie week may have allowed University of Manitoba students to flaunt their creativity and school spirit, but it also caused substantial traffic delays—especially as the parade always took place on a Friday evening. By the late 1960s, the parade was accompanied by complaints from business owners along the parade route, who blamed the parade for a reduction in customers. The annual tradition ended quietly in 1971.

Freshie Week was not the only time Winnipeg's downtown was awash with university students. Following a win from the University of Manitoba's football team, The Bisons, revelers amassed downtown. The 22-8 victory against the University of Saskatoon's Huskies, marked the end of a fourteen-year losing streak, so spirits were high. Students returning from Saskatoon on the C.P.R. line formed a conga line that snaked south on Main Street towards Portage Avenue. It ended at Portage and Main, where students stood outside the Bank of Montreal and chanted Bison songs. The proceedings managed to block *both* north- and south-bound traffic and led to the arrests of four students (who were later released without being charged). Despite this, it did not net major media coverage, existing only as a dramatized anecdote in *The Manitoban.*

Royal Visits

Every now and again, Winnipeg found the rare opportunity to resume jaywalking across Portage and Main. In 1951, a Royal Tour across Canada provided another opportunity. This was to be the first time in over a decade that the Royal Family had come to visit Winnipeg. King George VI had come in for a highly anticipated Canadian tour in 1939, just two years after his coronation. For King George VI, and his wife Queen Elizabeth, Winnipeg's Playhouse Theatre had organized a "Cavalcade of Welcome"— a pageant depicting Manitoba's history, culture, and loyalty to the crown. George Waight, who would go on to serve on the Victory Loans Committee, was on the Cavalcade Committee and the narrator for the production. A parade had been organized in their honour, too, with thousands crowding around Portage and Main to catch a glimpse of the couple driving by in their motorcade. The *Winnipeg Tribune* even published a photobook documenting the cross-country tour.

By 1951, though, King George's health had worsened. A 1949 tour to Australia and New Zealand had to be postponed due to an arterial blockage in his leg, and following this Princess Elizabeth and her husband Philip, Duke of Edinburgh, took over touring duties. When the time came to visit Canada in '51, it was Elizabeth and Philip who did so—though the trip was delayed by a week due to a setback in George's health.

When the royal couple did arrive, it was in mid-October on a crisp two-degree morning. A procession from the airport took them through the heart of Winnipeg and streets decorated with union jacks and pennant flags. Though these decorations were blocked by the masses of people gathering on the sidewalks. "Every means were put to use by the crowds. Stepladders, tail-gates of trucks, bumpers of cars, lamp posts and construction scaffolding were loaded with people trying to get a good view."[233]

At Portage and Main, people had climbed onto telephone poles, waste baskets, and signboards. Despite the efforts of the police to corral the public, the constant jostling pushed people into the street. Traffic was at a near standstill as a result, with police cars and motorcycle escorts left trying to push slowly through throngs of people. After fifteen minutes, order was restored and the royal procession continued on its way. The crowd dissipated, going back to their offices or to their homes, walking straight down the middle of Portage Avenue and oblivious to red lights. But then life returned to normal, and regular road rules applied. Not that everyone was in awe of the direction Winnipeg's traffic planning had taken.

When British architect Sir Hugh Casson attended the University of Manitoba Festival of Arts in 1959, he spoke unfavourably about the designs of Winnipeg streets. Speaking to a group of students and professors on November 9, he said: "The city belongs to the pedestrian. There must be ruthless segregation of motorists. It's an injustice when a pedestrian—on foot, in the cold, with three screaming kids—has to wait for a motorist, sitting in the [warmth]. When you walk, look. The man on the street now is a walking corpse. He hasn't looked at the city for years. He invades it every day, but he lives in subtopia."

He was even harsher about Winnipeg's major intersection: "Is Portage and Main the heart of your city? What did I find there? Nothing! Worse than nothing. An advertising sign as wide as this room. It's shameful."[234]

The 77 Steps

Casson's ideas were ones that might have been echoed by some of the regular patrons at Childs restaurant. With its long marble counter, black and white checkered floors, and mirror covered pillars, the restaurant had become an unlikely hot spot for Winnipeg's intellectual community in the late 1940s, a place to gather and lament that they did not live in a more cosmopolitan city. Tom Hendry, one of the regulars, described it as a place "for a few harried souls then managing the cultural ramparts out here in the artistic outback."[235]

The 'harried souls' holding down the fort were an impressive bunch. Co-inventor of Imax and award-winning documentarian Roman Kroitor, Governor General Award-winning artist Takao Tanabe, and authors Margaret Laurence and Adele Wisemen could often be found sipping ten-cent coffee at one of the marble-topped tables. It was Wiseman who would introduce Hendry and John Hirsch at Childs and start off a friendship and creative partnership that would radically change the world of Winnipeg theatre.

Hirsch, a Jewish-Hungarian refugee who had arrived in Winnipeg has part of Canada's War Orphan Program, saw opportunity in Winnipeg's starving creative scene—both as a form of healing for himself, and as a way of giving back to "the community that had adopted him."[236]

An unknown buyer had purchased the old Dominion Theatre on Portage Avenue East, and the Winnipeg Little Theatre had the option to take on the lease. Unknown to everyone at the time was that the buyer was Kathleen Richardson, who had met Hirsch when he'd applied for financial support from the Junior League to fund a children's puppet theatre in the early 1950s. Both Hirsch and Hendry contributed $2,000 to the project, with the remainder contributed by a friend, and Theatre 77 was formed.

The company name came from the theatre's proximity to Portage and Main, though the exact distance was a subject of debate. During an interview with Hirsch, *Winnipeg Free Press* reporter Frank Morris was told that

The interior of Childs Restaurant c. 1950
Archives of Manitoba

Tom Hendry had completed the journey in seventy-seven steps to "prove how convenient the theatre is to the hub of everything." Actor Moray Sinclair took longer, at 103 steps, and ballerina and Royal Winnipeg Ballet founder Betty Farraly managed an impressive seven. Ultimately, after a heated debate, Hirsch and Morris took to the street to settle the matter themselves. In the first attempt, Hirsch took eighty steps. In the second, Hirsch took seventy-seven—though Morris noted that Hirsch had "lengthened his steps, timing it so that it came to exactly 77."[237]

The name stuck, regardless of its accuracy. The following year, The-

The Dominion Theatre before and after renovations, in 1941 and 1957
Winnipeg Tribune Photo Collection, University of Manitoba Archives

atre 77 would merge with the Winnipeg Little Theatre to create the first regional theatre company in Canada: The Manitoba Theatre Centre, which ran productions out of Theatre 77 for the following decade. Hendry and Hirsch had a talented roster of local performers to recruit from—including Newfoundland-born Gordon Pinsent. Childs Restaurant, where Hirsch and Hendry had met, became a regular spot for performers to go following their shows.

Over the following decade, the Manitoba Theatre Centre would develop a reputation for high-quality entertainment in Winnipeg even if the Dominion Theatre sometimes failed to impress. A roof leak the first year threatened operations. Kathleen Richardson, interviewed for the John

Hirsch biography *A Fiery Soul*, lamented, "The ink was hardly dry on my having bought the wretched thing when the roof needed to be replaced."[238] Still, for a 1910s theatre with bandaged basement pipes that leaked during rehearsal, the theatre did well. But it was not to last forever.

A new construction boom was underway, a new attempt at modernizing a downtown that people felt was increasingly outdated—and Portage and Main was to play a key role in this reshaping of Winnipeg.

Chapter 7
Closing the Corner

Winnipeg's downtown was dying.

It is an old refrain, going back to the 1950s, when downtown residents began moving out towards surrounding suburban municipalities. Between 1941 and 1966, Winnipeg's downtown population declined 44%, with regional populations increasing 68% —leaving an increasingly vacant downtown. The problem was not unique to Winnipeg: most North American cities faced some form of the same problem in the period following World War Two. Across the continent, urban planners and government officials were trying to reimagine the idea of a successful and vibrant city with varying degrees of success.

In Winnipeg, the development of the Metropolitan Corporation in 1961 made success difficult. The Metro Corp, was responsible for a lot of civic management that took place in and between the communities: planning roads, bridge crossings, park developments, water and sewage services, and even transit. It was also a remarkably bloated institution and was made up of representatives from Winnipeg's core area and the twelve surrounding municipalities—Brooklands, Charleswood, Tuxedo, Transcona, West Kildonan, North Kildonan, East Kildonan, Old Kildonan, Saint Boniface, Saint Vital, St. James, and Fort Garry. Involved were 112 mayors, reeves, councillors and aldermen, and 85 school trustees, totaling 197 representatives for a population of around 550,000. With so many voices involved, lines between who was responsible for what, and who *should* be responsible grew increasingly fuzzy.

Representatives for the surrounding municipalities wanted funds directed towards their communities, leaving less money for Winnipeg's downtown where many area residents continued to work, shop, and play—just not live. The age of downtown buildings was also a point of concern. The 1960s was not a golden era of historic preservation, especially for a city desperately keen to prove itself a modern one. A study from the time found that around two-thirds of downtown buildings were not suited for new development.[239]

Going Up, Going Down

It was clear at the time that new developments were necessary. Even Eaton's Department Store had an opinion on the matter, running a 1968 exhibit called "Project Tomorrow." Here, one could see "outstanding displays of transportation in the world of tomorrow, the fashions you'll wear tomorrow, and the houses you'll live in." The exhibit also highlighted the trends in urban design in Winnipeg, such as skywalk passages connecting downtown buildings—and tidily expressed the sentiment towards older architecture. "In Winnipeg—the City of Tomorrow—away with the ugly old, and in with the beautifully functional, through the new wonders of inspired town planning and urban renewal."[240] One specific new development was the main focus of the exhibit: Lombard Place.

The project was announced in late 1965, after James Richardson and Sons had spent months quietly purchasing a number of surrounding properties to accommodate the massive development plan. The company was revisiting the idea of a massive office tower at Portage and Main, this time minus the gothic trappings of their 1920s plan. The new improved Richardson building was to be a thirty-four-storey office tower, designed by architecture firm Smith Carter Parkin. A hotel, at 2 Lombard Place, was to be built next door—necessitating the demolition of the Dominion Theatre and several other buildings along Main Street and Lombard Avenue.[241]

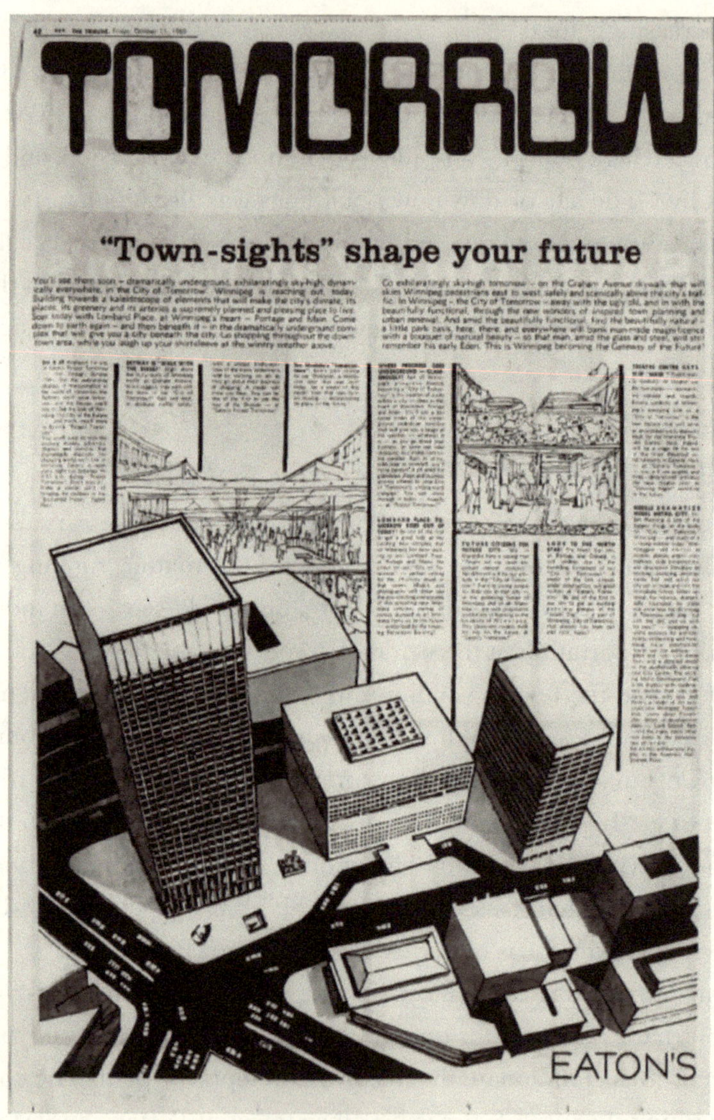

An advertisement for a 'City of Tomorrow,' with a rough outline of 1 & 2 Lombard Place and illustrations of an underground concourse

"The City of Tomorrow," October 11, 1968 Winnipeg Tribune Archives/University of Manitoba

Completion of the Richardson Building was a technical feat. It was Winnipeg's highest tower, beating the Childs building by twenty storeys. Local papers eagerly covered the building's construction. When the project was nearly complete in the fall of 1969, the *Winnipeg Tribune* published a photograph of the intersection with the Manitoba granite-clad skyscraper front and centre. Coming soon, "The West's Largest Windbreak."[242]

Phase two of the plan was the construction of a hotel next door, at 2 Lombard Place. Opened as the Winnipeg Inn, now the Fairmont, it was built to address a demand for accommodation in the growing conference industry. Estimates from the Manitoba travel and Convention Association stated that about 35,430 delegates had attended conventions in Winnipeg in 1968, with numbers expected to grow as Canada and Manitoba's centennials drew nearer.

The Winnipeg Inn, a joint venture between Lombard Place and Western International Hotels would add 350 new rooms, as well as convention space for 1,250. There was also local entertainment, at the Stage Door, and fine dining at the Velvet Glove, whose design was based on eighteenth-century Georgian stylings. Standards for the staff were strict: they were to leave through a side entrance, no snacks, candy, or food were allowed while working, and public spaces for guests were off-limits without prior permission (including public washrooms). These were uncommon regulations for a Winnipeg hotel and much more in line with accommodations found in places like New York and London.[243]

For all the glamour of the Winnipeg Inn and the promise of the new Richardson Building, the real excitement was underground. A proposed underground pedestrian concourse beneath 1 and 2 Lombard Place had captured the attention of city and metro planners, who were exploring all-weather pedestrian routes. The goal was to increase pedestrian traffic downtown by creating a series of skywalks and tunnels, so that people could move freely, unimpeded by inclement weather.

Early visions of the concourse saw it as step one of a larger plan to create an all-weather underground shopping mall that was massive in scope. It would span nearly two kilometers from City Hall on Main Street to the University of Winnipeg on Portage Avenue. To start, though, it would be a series of shops beneath the Richardson building, accessible by the office tower, the Winnipeg Inn, or the plaza outside. There were thoughts of extending the concourse to the other corners of the intersection to enable pedestrian crossing, though in 1968 these ideas were largely hypothetical.

What would happen *beyond* that initial concourse was a matter of debate. The Metro Corporation, which had approved of the concourse design, certainly had grand ambitions. Winnipeg's mayor Stephen Juba had other plans.

Winnipeg vs. Metro

Stephen Juba, by this point, had been mayor of Winnipeg for a decade and had established a pattern of outlandish behaviour. Journalist Paul Gresco summed it up nicely: "Be jealously protective of the city's reputation, pick an easily identifiable issue, attack a single recognizable enemy, use an outlandish gimmick that will attract the attention of photographers, and raise an outrageous ruckus that will command headlines."[244]

The Winnipeg Metropolitan Corporation was a frequent target of Juba's ire, one that he had in fact campaigned on dissolving. Juba, through the City of Winnipeg, sparred with Metro on all things planning. Taxes, roads, water, anything involved in municipal affairs they likely fought about. In a 1965 debate with Metro chairman Richard Bonnycastle, Juba said of Metro: "We need it like a hole in the head."[245] So, if the Metro was proposing going underground, Juba would suggest something different.

His idea was the total opposite of Metro's: a second-storey walkway/mall that would sit above Graham Avenue. Admittedly, it wasn't one of Juba's better schemes. The mechanics of it had yet to be worked out, for one thing. "The plaza itself probably would be built with concrete decks supported across, and from roof to ground, by steel

A 1970 advertisement mocking Juba and Metro's ongoing battles over control of downtown
Winnipeg Tribune, August 27, 1970 Winnipeg Tribune Archives/University of Manitoba

girders."[246] Carbon monoxide from the cars below was a point of concern, as was acquiring the air rights above Graham Avenue.

Representatives from Metro brushed Juba off. "I don't think he's really serious about the development," Charles Hubbard, vice-chairman of Metro said. "First he gets his own administration to attack Metro's proposal for an underground shopping mall at Portage and Main and then he hoists this idea."[247]

Hubbard was referring to a report published by Winnipeg engineer W.D. Hurst criticizing the potential high costs of the project and the additional price of relocating utilities. There was, too, the concern over *who* had rights to the space below the street. Metro was able to develop Winnipeg streets, but it was up to the province to decide whether Metro was also entitled to use the ground below.

Ultimately, the province gave the project the go-ahead, despite the efforts of Juba. The novelty of the location did attract tenants from a wide array of businesses. Some early occupants of the Lombard Place underground mall included Laura Secord Chocolatier, Margie's Legworks, Jerome Rochetti's Wigtowne, and Cafe Lombard. Business was slow, at first, but tenants were hopeful things would pick up as more people learned how to access the space.

In the midst of the Lombard Place project, other plans were being made for the rest of the downtown area. Removing the streetcars tracks had not eased congestion in the long-term, and once again downtown Winnipeg was being overrun with backed-up traffic and frustrated motorists. A lack of new development, low land values, and a central business area that was nearly 40% surface parking lots were all symptoms of larger problem. And while Juba may have had ideas for saving downtown, the City of Winnipeg itself lacked a planning department. Metro had one. Over the course of the 1960s, Metro would produce a series of planning documents detailing both present and potential future problems. One solution, put forward in the Winnipeg Area Transportation Study, suggested creating 119 miles of new roads and expressways to accommodate what they predicted would be a massive jump in car usage. The Downtown Development Plan proposed separating pedestrians from cars vertically and transforming back alleys into enclosed indoor malls.

Parking was a continual problem. Surface parking lots did not bring in tax revenue for the city, and the difficulty of finding parking was a deterrent for those trying to come downtown. Enclosed parking garages caught the attention of both Metro and the City, though there was difficulty finding funds without the support of a development company or business. Unfortunately, as Stephen Juba would announce at a Parking Authority meeting in 1968, interested developers were hesitant to build downtown due to a lack of parking. Here, again, Juba found a chance to combat Metro.

If it was parking developers wanted, well, why not underneath Portage and Main? Sure, that was where Metro was considering building a pedes-

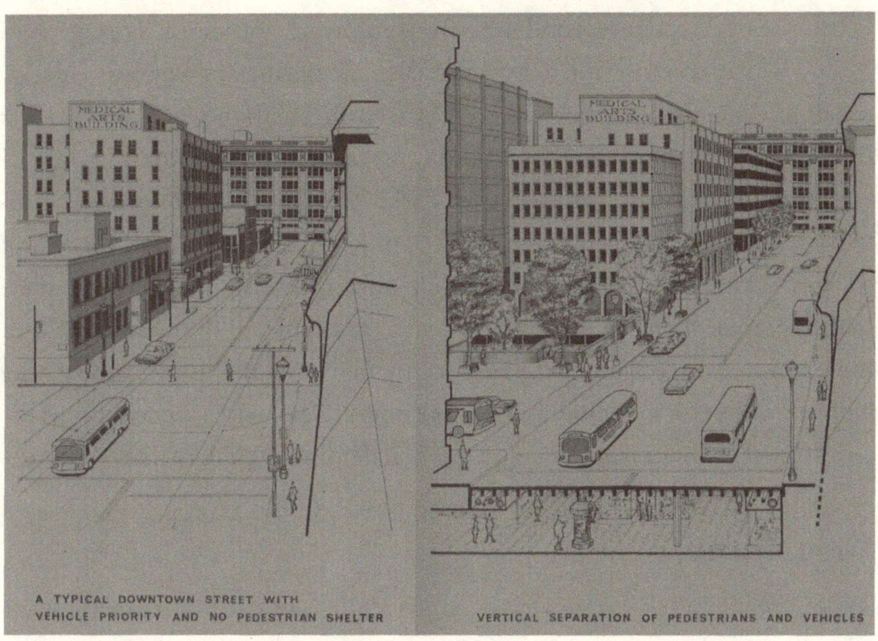

A plate from the Downtown Development Plan depicting two versions of Graham Avenue
Plate 22 Winnipeg Planning Division, Winnipeg Planning Division, 1966 City of Winnipeg Archives

trian concourse, but that was all the more reason to push ahead. Despite Metro setting aside $400,000 for the project, Hurst pushed back—arguing that Metro might not have the right to build underground, and that, as a city engineer, he thought the project was too dangerous. Juba, less eloquently, called those who supported the concourse over his parking garage plan "Stupid."[248]

Metro backed off the concourse idea by 1970, while the Winnipeg Parking Authority moved forward with their plans to develop new parking garages with the full support of city council. A by-law to expropriate two tracts of land to develop new parking garages was passed on July 27, 1970, in record speed for a council meeting. The whole process took less than half an hour.

The first site was north of Portage Avenue, between Hargrave and

Carlton Streets. The second was the southwest corner of Portage and Main, which was occupied by several small businesses but was, like so much of downtown, largely covered by a surface parking lot. Metro called the decision 'retrogressive,' but there was nothing to be done.[249]

Architectural firm Smith Carter Parkin was hired to submit a site evaluation to the city. This was the same firm to develop Lombard Place and to work with Metro on the concourse plans, so they had some experience with the area. Their advice was to focus on multi-use development, with the parking garage built as the first component. All of this was proceeding without a developer being named, but there was one in mind: the Montreal-based Trizec Properties, Inc, on behalf of the Bank of Nova Scotia.

Enter, Trizec

Trizec, which had been in business since 1960, had made a name for itself with the development of Place Ville Marie in Montreal. In fact, when planning for the concourse, Metro officials had gone to visit Montreal for inspiration and information.

Likely Trizec had begun exploring the idea of moving to Winnipeg sometime before 1970, though there is no written evidence of contact between the organization and Winnipeg's city council. Interviews with those involved in 1976 indicate that Juba and Metro Chairman Jack Willis had separately reached out to Trizec at some point around 1971. No real progress could be made until 1972. The province announced plans to eliminate Metro on January 1, 1972—with a municipal election called for October of 1971. Juba was in the running, of course, as were Willis and Metro council member Bill Hutton. Willis and Hutton were both opposed to the parking garage scheme; Hutton called it "Stupider than Stupid" at one point.

Juba won the election handily.

With Winnipeg now managed by a municipal Unicity government, led by

Mayor Juba, development could continue without the two organizations butting heads. And Juba was keen to see the Trizec deal through—so was Trizec's president, Jim Soden. Described as a "burly, determined-looking individual" with a "non-conforming hairstyle," he was a lawyer turned property developer with Trizec who was working hard to sell their vision for Winnipeg.[250] When presenting his ideas to the City, Soden went direct to Juba. Among the conditions which stipulated the buildings' floor area, air rights and parking stalls for tenants Soden made the following requests:

1. A 99-year lease
2. Free rent for the first two years following the completion of the 1,000-car parking garage.
3. No rent increase for the first forty years.

These would be, effectively, the same terms the city council would agree to. A few detractors would point out that the contract included an escape clause for Trizec but not for the city itself, but they were outvoted. Others pointed out that there was no deadline for Trizec to complete the project. And, further, as a bargaining chip the city had agreed to cover the expropriation costs. Progress was slow, even after a memorandum of agreement was signed. A proper deal wouldn't be reached until 1974, all the while the city worked fervently to entice Trizec to build.

In the interim, Montreal urban planner Vincent Ponte was brought in to conceptualize a plan for the intersection. It did not take long for Ponte to conclude that pedestrians and traffic had to be separated, but his means of doing so were too elaborate for Winnipeg. His first proposal was an elevated saucer, supported eighteen feet above traffic, but this was dismissed by both the Richardson Building and the Bank of Montreal. His second idea, construction of an underground passageway, would have sounded painfully familiar to Winnipeg's city council. But it was appealing to Trizec, and to the Richardson Building—especially as Ponte's vision of

The proposed Trizec design from 1976. In the end, only one tower would be completed.
Winnipeg Evening Tribune, June 3, 1976 Winnipeg Tribune Archives/University of Manitoba

the underground was a busy one. For $2.7 million, Ponte estimated 3,000 linear feet of retail stores with 22,000 pedestrians passing through daily.

Reporter Val Werier, in the *Winnipeg Tribune*, was optimistic about the opportunities the development could provide for Winnipeg's "No 1 corner."[251] As Trizec wouldn't announce its plans until late 1973, Werier imagined a Portage and Main with a public plaza, full of greenery. It was a chance to change the intersection's cold and windy reputation for a "much happier reputation as being a place for people."[252]

An agreement was finally reached between the City of Winnipeg in January of 1974, approved by a vote of 21 to 12—with seventeen councillors absent. Trizec proposed building two office towers, rising thirty-four storeys, a regional bank for the Bank of Nova Scotia, a large shopping mall and a hotel. The cost for the project was estimated at around $80 million. This proposal, while presented to council, was not included as a requirement in the agreement—meaning that Trizec had no legal responsibility to actually complete the project as pitched to the city. The plans also projected a rentable area of around one million square feet, but Trizec refused to commit to building more than 300,000 square feet. The city, in return, would cover the costs of the land expropriation *and* the construction of a parking garage.

Council members who voted against the project were in agreement on one thing: the whole process had moved too quickly for anyone to comprehend it properly. Taxpayer money was on the hook for a project, with little to hold Trizec responsible too. Lord Selkirk Councillor Joseph Zuken was harsh in his delivery: "Trizec used high-skilled professionals who did a super pitch job on the city's administration, who are a bunch of amateurs."[253]

Work was already underway on the project by this point. Demolition had started in 1973, moving forward despite the concern of the Board of Commissioners. J.B. Demolitions had been hired by Trizec to do the work, but without a performance bond which would financially tie the contracting company to the project. "Trizec can take its chances on a contract with no performance bond, whereas the city can't," was the explanation of Chief Commissioner D.I. MacDonald.[254] Partial cost of the demolition, $52,000, would still fall to the city—paid directly to Trizec, who in turn, would pay J.B. Demolitions for the work.

All the buildings at that corner dated back to the turn of the twentieth century, a fact that was not lost on Winnipeg's nascent heritage preservation community. Randy Rostecki, who would later go on to prepare a document on the history of Portage and Main for the City of Winnipeg, wrote in to the *Winnipeg Tribune* to express concern that a developer like Trizec could have the City of Winnipeg expropriate buildings on their behalf. Further, in doing so, Winnipeg would "destroy many of our finer 1880s and early 1900s buildings for the sake of the almighty dollar."[255]

Among the buildings to be demolished were the Rowand Block, the old C.P.R. ticket office, the Bank of Ottawa and a second Bank of Montreal. Total preservation of the structures wasn't possible, nor were the developers particularly inclined to do so, but the Manitoba Historical Society was able to salvage parts of the buildings to be repurposed into the Bank of Nova Scotia and around Winnipeg Square. The archway from the William and Alloway Banking Hall was also saved and reused in the C.N. Railyard developments.

The southwest corner of Portage and Main before demolition
Winnipeg Tribune June 1, 1973 Winnipeg Tribune Archives/University of Manitoba

Another problem struck the development in late 1974: neither the City of Winnipeg nor Trizec had prepared a comprehensive environmental impact report on the parking garage. President of Winnipeg Pollution Probe David Miles brought this fact to the attention of council—and threatened a lawsuit over the violation of 653 of the City Act. This was a new Act in the country, and Winnipeg had just enacted it during Unicity in 1972. It meant that every new project proposal for public works was meant to consider: "a) the environmental impact of the proposed work, b) any adverse environment effects which cannot be avoided should the work be undertaken and c) alternatives to the proposed action," but in the case of the Trizec deal it had been overlooked. Further construction would have to

Saving the Alloway and Champion
Photographer Gregg Burner, *Winnipeg Tribune* April 24, 1975 Winnipeg Tribune Archives/University of Manitoba

stop until the situation was remedied. Miles had stumbled across a public advocacy landmine. Winnipeg Pollution Probe and the Manitoba Environmental Council held meetings to discuss the topic, both among each other and directly with city council. Dr. Jennifer Shay, with the Manitoba Environmental Council, argued that the parking structure had not met *any* of the ten established development guidelines and that, overall, "the review does not cover much of anything; it is primarily descriptive rather than analytical."[256]

The city settled out-of-court with Miles and were forced to draw up a proper environmental impact statement that reached council by February 1975. While it was *hoped* that the city could reject proposals with poor impact studies, the letter of the law did not force them to do so—and council had no intention of changing that. An Executive Policy Committee on February 27, 1975, saw mayor and council cracking jokes at the expense of a nervous city clerk, who tripped over his words presenting an environmental impact statement to them, and making repeated quips about the perceived absurdity of the law. A motion to *repeal* City Act 653 was even put forward, as politicians worried the act would stall all new developments. Winnipeg's policy committee would, in light of this and a later trilevel report, look into creating a much smaller parking lot than the promised thousand-car garage.

Environmental policies weren't the only thing slowing the project down. Trizec was having difficulties finding tenants for their office tower. Great West Life, which Soden had hoped would move into the tower, had instead opted to work with C.N. Rail on the East Railyard development scheme that would ultimately become The Forks. There had also been plans for a hotel in the building, but Winnipeg's high-end hotel market was oversaturated as it was, and no hotelier could be found to operate out of the Trizec building. The longer it took to find interested tenants, the more difficult it was to attract people to the project at all. Trizec was not a small company, however, and it could afford to wait it out. This was less of a luxury for the city, who had invested significant time and money already.

To start, legal fees from the expropriation were significantly higher than expected. Just the cost of the land alone was $1.3 million an acre, not including legal fees and demolition costs. The initial project budget, for just the parking garage was $5 million.

In an effort to alleviate corporate concerns, Stephen Juba wrote to Soden to express interest in some civic offices occupying the building. A delegation of city politicians had also gone to Ottawa to convince the federal government to invest in the development. It was not enough for Trizec to move forward. When demolitions were completed in 1975, Trizec had the lot covered in gravel.

Like the rest of downtown, part of Portage and Main had been turned into a surface parking lot.

In this political cartoon, Henry McKenney is proposing his vision for the future of Portage and Main—a fenced off construction site.
Jan Kamienski, *Winnipeg Tribune* April 22, 1976 Winnipeg Tribune Archives/University of Manitoba

Breaking Ground

Unsurprisingly, some felt it was time for the city to jump ship.

A 1975 tri-level government task force, tasked with determining priorities for downtown development, recommended totally abandoning the project. Instead, it suggested that federal public works build a 600,000 square foot structure—double the size of what Trizec had promised. On the whole, the report was the exact opposite of Juba's vision of downtown. Prepared by city planners from all levels of government, the task force's report suggested creating new apartments downtown and prioritizing public transit at the express expense of cars, which "must be discouraged within downtown Winnipeg."[257] The Winnipeg Chamber of Commerce also voiced their displeasure, blaming city council for creating "a bleak, bare, ugly parking lot."[258]

A *Free Press* editorial was even more scathing, with a full page criticizing the project—with the headline: "Handling development: is the city in Blunderland?"[259] Even council had turned. In a *Free Press* poll, twenty-six councillors expressed that they felt the deal was a bad one, another twelve stayed silent on the matter. Only twelve were in Juba's corner and if the mayor had any doubts, he wasn't letting it show. Juba and Jim Soden were a united front on the development; it was a good deal, the development *would* happen, they were just waiting for the best time.

It was up to Soden and Trizec's board to determine what the best time would be. By 1976, plans for another underground concourse at Portage and Main were circulating once again. To build, the City's Chief Commissioner, D.I. MacDonald, would need permission from property owners on all four corners. Trizec's support was conditional: if the city would stick with the original thousand-car parking garage plan, Trizec would agree to the concourse.

In theory, the creation of a concourse was for pedestrian safety. Ad-hoc civic committees had been puzzling over how to mix cars and people at Portage and Main and had come to one solid conclusion: it couldn't be done. Barring pedestrian traffic at street level and building an underground walkway was the only reasonable solution. Civic affairs reporter Ron Kustra doubted the pedestrian safety angle:

> What the ad hoc committee doesn't say is that the concourse is especially important to the business situation on the four corners of the intersection and it is for their benefit—not the pedestrian—that the scheme is really being advanced. Lombard Place mall merchants, tenants of the Richardson Building, expected the concourse several years ago. One proprietor recently told a *Tribune* colleague the city's failure to funnel people under Portage and Main, and through the concourse, has meant subsidized rents from the Richardson Company. Still, several shopkeepers may be forced to close their doors anyway.[260]

If the purpose was truly economic, pedestrian safety was a clever cover, and funds to build it were approved in 1975—pending, of course, Trizec's permission. Council members were incredulous at the demand. Morris Kaufman, Councillor for Fort Rouge, said "when Soden tells the city to jump, they hold a meeting to ask him how high. He gets everything he asks, and then the city says what more?"[261]

Designs for the concourse, and the closed intersection, were put forward by Smith Carter Partners in June of 1976, envisioning shrubbery-covered barricades to prevent pedestrians from crossing the street. V.K. Mason Construction was then awarded the contract for concourse construction in December, to a council vote 24-19. At last a deal had *finally* been reached. The six property owners on all four corners had agreed to the construction of the concourse and had even agreed to cover one fifth of the costs. So as to "not short-circuit" the project, the city in turn agreed to close the street to pedestrians. It was a forty-year contract, subject in renewal 2016. Juba got his parking garage, MacDonald had gotten the concourse, and Trizec got one hell of a deal.

Juba would not stay in politics long enough to see the project completed. He lost the 1977 mayoral election to Robert Steen, after twenty years in the mayoral office. The political changeover did not significantly impact the Portage and Main development. True to plan, Portage and Main was closed for reconstruction on May 29, 1978, with a completion date of fall of that same year. A summer construction strike delayed the project for four and a half months and led to half a year's worth of complaints about delayed traffic due to lane closures. Once the strike resolved, the Winnipeg Square Parking Garage was completed first, at a cost of $8.2 million (nearly $400,000 over budget).

To celebrate the first phase of construction, the city held an opening ceremony with a twist. In lieu of a regular ribbon-cutting, parking authority chairman John Gee would crash a car straight through the garage's automatic door—which had, for the occasion, been replaced by a Styrofoam fake. Event organizers imagined the Styrofoam flying apart as Gee crashed through, to the astonishment of those assembled to watch. The Styrofoam was sturdier than expected. When Gee "rammed his car through the entrance, the painted Styrofoam just bent, and bent ... and bent." Once the car was through, it fell back into place as if nothing had happened. "Ah," a city official lamented aloud, "it was supposed to break."[262]

The audience applauded regardless. Mayor Steen delivered a quick address about the future of the development, joined by Trizec's new president Harold Milavsky. Both were optimistic about the first phase of the project— Trizec's first office tower— and vague about the start of phase two. There were vague plans for a second tower, a hotel, and maybe even an indoor garden—though none of this was official. It helped that Trizec had finally found a tenant for the tower, The Commodity Exchange, and were now anticipating opening around 1980—about ten years after the project began.

Completion of the concourse followed quickly after the parking garage. It was completed in February of 1979, an underground ring connecting the four corners of Portage and Main to each other. Running through the centre of the concourse was a massive piece of public art, designed by local sculptor Bruce Head. A graduate of the University of Manitoba's art school and graphic designer, Head was a contemporary artist whose design won the 1977 commission to build a new art piece for the concourse. It was an impressive undertaking, made up of fifty-two moulded concrete panels with abstract designs. Titled *The Wall*, it took Head two years to create—with many of the moulded panels being made on-site at the intersection.

There was a small window of time where pedestrians could still cross the street *and* the concourse was open. During this time, CBC Winnipeg reporter Terry Matte took to the corner to interview pedestrians—all of whom were braving February winds above ground. Matte stopped one man to ask, "How come you're going to walk across the street instead of the underground walkway?"

His response? "Because I don't know how to get to it just yet—and this is faster."

He was not the only one to have trouble finding the entrance. During the course of a very brief news segment, Matte had to point to it out to several more people. One woman gauged the distance, laughed, and told Matte: "Ah, it's kind of far. I think I'll just run across." A few happily took Matte's directions, ducking inside to escape the cold February winds.[263]

Construction of the concourse beneath the Bank of Montreal
Winnipeg Tribune Photo Collection, University of Manitoba Archives. December 17, 1977

A section of the Bruce Head sculpture in 2025
Alex Judge

On the whole, the public was not opposed to the concourse. What they were opposed to, however, was the decision to close the street to pedestrians. Val Werier, who had spent so much of the past decade writing about an intersection made for the public, was extremely vocal about his opinions. Alongside cartoonist Jan Kamienski, Werier wrote a series of articles from 1978 onwards criticizing all aspects of the development.

The barricades erected on street level were "ugly, and oppressive" even with shrubbery planted to cover them. [264] The labyrinthian design of the underground was also up for criticism. Another *Tribune* editorial described going into the concourse as scuttling "underground like timid gophers. We will trek past artful shop displays designed to part us and our dollars. We will, it is hoped, find the right staircase to reach the surface. If not, we must once more imitate the gophers, duck down and try again. Great, say the planners. Get those dopey pedestrians out of the way. Who needs them? Give traffic another break. Can't stand in the way of progress, baby."[265]

Councillor Joseph Zuken, one of a small few who had been against the Trizec deal since the beginning, had promised to hold a protest march

Two of Kamienski's cartoons critiquing the Trizec project

Jan Kamienski *Winnipeg Tribune* June 3, 1976 Winnipeg Tribune Archives/University of Manitoba

"Dear Winnipeg Citizen," Jan Kamienski *Winnipeg Tribune* February 22, 1979 Winnipeg Tribune Archives/University of Manitoba Archives if the intersection closed. He held true to his word, organizing a march on March 9, 1979. Joined by fifteen supporters, including three in wheelchairs and members of the Manitoba League of the Physically Handicapped, the group jaywalked across all four corners of Portage and Main. Another hundred people had gathered to watch, including reporters. The group's main issue was the lack of accessible entrances to the concourse. At the time, only two corners had elevator access: the Trizec Building and the Richardson Building. People crossing at Childs or the Bank of Montreal would have to walk down a flight of stairs which would become icy in the winters. Even accessing the escalators at Childs and the Bank of Montreal involved climbing a short flight of stairs. And, for pedestrians using wheelchairs or with mobility difficulties, Portage and Main abruptly became off-limits.

At least one councillor was opposed to Zuken's march. Don Smith, a former football player, threated to "meet Zuken in the middle of the street and carry him back." But another member of council came to express support. Morris Kauman, by this point a former councillor, offered to represent Zuken if the police chose to charge him with jaywalking.[266]

Zuken's protest was a one-day affair. There was another group much more dedicated to jaywalking. The Right to Walk Group, founded by Department of Social and Preventative Medicine professor Evelyn Shapiro, were engaged in "'guerrilla' tactics, climbing around or over the barriers and darting through heavy traffic to cross the street."[267] One observer, from a camera shop at the intersection, noted that most of the people he saw jaywalking were elderly. "One morning, I saw an old man almost get blown under the wheels of a truck."[268]

Zuken was quick to point out that, if the intent of the concourse was truly to improve pedestrian safety, council had erred along the way. He led another protest, on April 18, to convince council to reverse the decision—this time joined by fifty people. The Right to Walk had gained three hundred supporters by this time, though a lack of support from the property

Joseph Zuken leading a protest walking across Portage and Main, September 3, 1979
Winnipeg Tribune Photo Collection, University of Manitoba Archives

owners at Portage and Main meant the movement never progressed past 1980. Werier had also taken up the cause, interviewing Winnipeggers with disabilities and advocating for changes at the corner whenever the topic came up.

Construction carried on at Portage and Main throughout this. On July 24, 1980, Trizec's Commodity Exchange Building officially opened. It was a 31-storey, $35 million, office tower. The Bank of Nova Scotia occupied part of the first floor, in a glass-covered office reminiscent of a greenhouse. Set back slightly was a tower, angled so that the façade directly faced Portage and Main. The Commodity Exchange's offices, on the third and fourth floors, were fully modern, complete with a computerized trading floor. Manitoba Agriculture Minister Jim Downey was present to explain how everyone would work to a crowd of about 350 people, but he was drowned out by pre-recorded "shouts of traders, played through the sound system to add authenticity to the proceedings."[269]

The building's tenants were indicative of Manitoba's economy. Insurance firms, stock traders, and agricultural companies made up the bulk of the occupants. Canada Malting Limited had even installed a barley sorting facility in the building. Below, in Trizec's underground mall, remnants of former buildings were scattered throughout.

Learning from the Past

Mistakes had been made. Most were able to admit that by 1980. The city had been too hasty to attract a new developer and had overlooked a number of red flags. Trizec, for example, had never owned the land during the development process. The initial 1972 contract did not force Trizec to commit to their initial development idea either.

With no financial stake and no legal obligations, Trizec had minimal risks while the city shouldered the bulk of the costs. And, in the end, the Trizec never built the second tower or the hotel. It is not totally clear how much the entire process cost the city; estimates put it around $35 million. Laying the blame at Trizec's feet would be the easiest option, but the fact of the matter is Winnipeg's government was scrambling for *anything* that could save a declining downtown. While Trizec may have been the catalyst for closing the intersection for pedestrians, it was not the first time the idea had been suggested. Metro chairman Jack Willis had suggested it in 1971 when the concourse and shopping mall was being developed. Even back then, Val Werier had been critical of the matter:

> However, I would like to make a plea that instead of banning pedestrians that we ban the cars. Instead of designing a city based on the needs of the car, we should think of people. Unless some dramatic action is taken in these terms, Winnipeg will be like the other large centers where the car determines the downtown character. There is nothing wrong itself in the idea of a Portage and Main Underground connection. But there must be a broader concept as well of how Winnipeg wants to treat pedestrians and motorists.

"If anything is to be banned," concluded Werier, "it should be the cars. After all, people are far more interesting."

Chapter 8

Making an Icon

It was, of course, people that created Portage and Main's mythology. Protests and celebrations had centred it as a gathering place, while stories and song had cemented it as a part of Winnipeg's lore. By the 1980s, the intersection was completely unrecognizable. The northwest corner, with its cluster of smaller structures (including Childs) was demolished to make way for the TD Tower, now 201 Portage, between 1988-1990. The architecture that had defined the skyline was vanishing in the name of progress—all, that is, but one building. The Bank of Montreal was not just standing; it had undergone a massive renovation to modernize aspects while leaving much of the historical character intact.

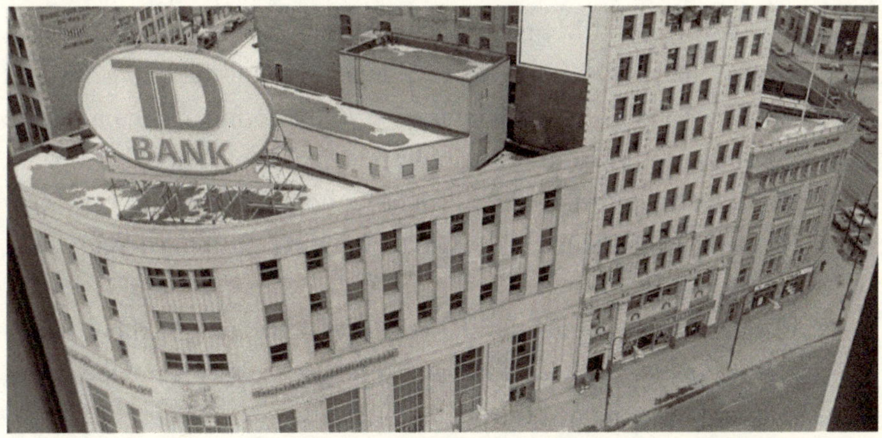

The northwest corner of Portage and Main in 1976
Jim Walker, Winnipeg Tribune Fonds, University of Manitoba Archives

It was an unusual decision at the time, especially for Portage and Main. Nearly a decade after Trizec, the oldest structures on the corner were slated for demolition to make way for another office tower. According to some, like University of Winnipeg professor David Walker, Winnipeg had failed to learn from its mistakes. "Municipal politicians feel that if they don't make a move, they'll miss the boat," he explained to the *Winnipeg Free Press.* "As a result, they have no vision about the future of development in Winnipeg."[270]

The increase in demolitions had rallied a motley crew of advocates together as early as 1978. Heritage preservation, or the protection of Winnipeg's historic buildings, was a new idea at the time. The construction of the Trizec building had caused the demolition of four structures on the southeast corner already, and in 1978 the city announced new plans to demolish the Canadian Bank of Commerce and the Bank of Hamilton just north of the intersection on Main Street. The new plan to replace these massive banking halls? Another parking lot.

David McDowell, president of the Manitoba Historical Society organized a protest beginning at the Richardson Building. In a 2018 speech, he recalled painting placards in his basement along with other protestors. McDowell, armed with a bullhorn, led the group on the chilly walk from Portage and Main north down Main Street, past the threatened banking halls all the way to City Hall. Out of this protest would come the creation of Heritage Winnipeg in 1978. Both banking halls were saved, preserving part of the original architecture of Winnipeg's Main Street. Heritage Winnipeg, alongside the Manitoba Historical Society, criticized the decision to demolish the Childs Building, but new development once again won out.

And yet, without the turn-of-the-century architecture, without streetcars bustling down the tracks, and even without people crossing the street, Portage and Main remained the heart of the city.

David McDowell leading heritage protest in 1978
Winnipeg Tribune Photo Collection, University of Manitoba Archives

The Best Game You Can Name

Pedestrians may not have been crossing the street on a day-to-day basis, but some remnant of those earlier large celebrations at the corner remained.

Most sports celebrations were spur-of-the-moment affairs, with the exception of one: the signing of Bobby Hull. In 1971, the Winnipeg Jets were a founding franchise in the World Hockey Association, and owner Ben Hatskin was working on assembling a world-class team. Veteran player Norm Beaudin was the first to be signed after over a decade playing for various teams across North America. Hull came second, in a massive ceremony that took place outside Portage and Main. This was in 1972, before the intersection had closed to the public, so traffic was blocked for the event. Getting Hull to play for Winnipeg was a massive success on the part of Hatskin, who had to convince Hull to leave the NHL to join the new league.

With the NHL, Hull had amassed an impressive record as a left-wing player with a record-breaking fifty-four goals in a season. Having him for the Jets would be a huge win in legitimizing the new team, so Hatskin put significant effort and money into recruiting him. Months of negotiations, with competing offers from the Chicago Blackhawks, meant that signing Hull would cost $3 million. In Hatskin's opinion, it was money well spent. Contracts went back and forth until it came time for a final signing, which would be a scheduled public ceremony at 5 p.m. on June 27, 1972.

Hatskins and Hull at Portage and Main
Winnipeg Tribune, June 28, 1972 Winnipeg Tribune Archive/University of Manitoba

A warm reception was waiting for Hull and Hatskin at Portage and Main. Three thousand people were gathered around, blocking off rush hour traffic for half an hour. The final signing took place on stage, followed by brief speeches from politicians and finally from Hull. He'd been given a good contract, much higher than anyone expected from a new sports league. His ten-year contract with the World Hockey Association included both a hefty signing bonus of $1 million dollars and an annual salary for $250,000.

Hull, who today has a legacy as a great hockey player and deeply flawed individual, was one third of the Winnipeg Jets' 'Hot Line' alongside players Anders Bedberg and Ulf Nilsson. Together, they led the Jets to win the Avco Cup three times. Following their first in 1976, a parade was planned in the team's honour—it culminated at Portage and Main, on the spot where Hull had signed on four years earlier. Winnipeggers were ecstatic. Mayor Stephen Juba declared May 28th Winnipeg Jets Day, and thousands lined Portage Avenue to catch a glimpse of the team or the cup.

Celebrating the AVCO Cup at Portage and Main May 28, 1976
Winnipeg Tribune Photo Collection, University of Manitoba Archives

While the WHA was short-lived, the Jets managed to be one of the most successful teams within the league. So much so that when the NHL and WHA merged, the Winnipeg Jets were one of four teams to transfer over. This lasted until 1996, when rising costs led to the Jets relocating to Arizona and becoming the Phoenix Coyotes.

The significance of Hull's signing stuck around, though, long enough that when it was announced that the Atlanta Thrashers would be transferring to Winnipeg in 2011, people returned to the same site. The Winnipeg Jets, in a new form, were coming back. It was announced at a morning press conference on Tuesday, May 31 with Winnipeg businessman Mark Chipman, NHL commissioner Gary Bettman, and Premier Greg Selinger. Roughly a thousand Winnipeggers were at Portage and Main waiting on the news. Some stood on the concrete barricades, bracing themselves against the wind, while others took to playing a game of street hockey in the intersection. Two fans brought in chairs from the old Winnipeg Arena to watch the proceedings. Winnipeg police officers were on standby, suggesting fans head to the celebrations taking place at the Forks instead. "For safety concerns and just practicality," police spokesperson Jason Michalyshen said, "Portage and Main is not the best place for that."[271]

Neither of these were points of concern for hockey fans in 2018, a hockey season that saw the Winnipeg Jets reach the NHL playoffs. Massive 'Whiteout' parties were planned for downtown, taking up stretches of the streets just south of Portage Avenue. With each win, excitement intensified, culminating in two Whiteout parties taking over Portage and Main. The first, following a 5-0 victory against the Minnesota Wild, took place in April. The second came in May, following a Game 7 win. And, in the middle of the two, Winnipeg's Bhangra Club recorded a video of their members dancing outside the Richardson Building clad in Jets jerseys and holding hockey sticks. While the Jets did not win the Stanley Cup, Portage and Main was cemented as an important part of the Jets legacy.

There was similar enthusiasm for Winnipeg's two Grey Cup wins

Jets fans celebrating at Portage and Main in 2011
Mike Deal/Winnipeg Free Press

in 2019 and 2021. The first marked the Blue Bombers first CFL win in twenty-nine years, and supporters flooded the streets of downtown Winnipeg—armed with footballs and miniature Grey Cups. Photos and videos on social media show riotously happy crowds, chanting and singing and celebrating together. As the 2020 CFL season was called off due to the COVID-19 pandemic, the 2021 Grey Cup win marked two consecutive victories from the Blue Bombers. And once more, people rushed to Portage and Main. With COVID restrictions still in place, numbers at the second gathering were smaller than the first, but the mood was still high.

Interestingly, Portage and Main also had a role to play in earlier Blue Bombers history. In 1980, as part of a Blue Bombers 50th birthday celebration, Mayor Bill Norrie organized a ceremonial kickoff at the intersection. On June 10, Portage Avenue was temporarily renamed Bomber Way. A procession of former players, coaches, bands, and mascots made their way down Portage and Main, which, as a treat, had been reopened to pedestrians for one hour only. Norrie and other dignitaries were there to host the kickoff. Yes, the *Winnipeg Tribune* joked, Joseph Zuken would finally get his chance to cross the intersection.

A Musical Icon

Across Winnipeg's lengthy and impressive musical history, Portage and Main has earned itself a number of mentions from high profile performers. Both Stompin' Tom Connors and Stan Rogers brought the intersection up in songs about the Prairies ("Red River Jane," for Connors, and "Free in the Harbour" for Rogers). Both men, while not from Winnipeg, were singers noted for their ability to capture and create Canadian identity. Even outside of Manitoba, Portage and Main was a defining element of the city.

It was an element that local performers also recognized. By 1975, Burton Cummings had left the Guess Who and left Winnipeg to pursue a solo career. He had not cut off Winnipeg entirely, returning to perform at the new Centennial Concert Hall for new album releases, and in 1979 Cummings came back from Los Angeles to record a CBC special: *Burton Cummings' Portage and Main*.

The program, written by Stan Jacobson, Paul Perlove, and a pre-SCTV Rick Moranis, saw Cummings performing with his first band, the Deverons, at their old high school and reuniting with the other members of the Guess Who (minus Jim Hale), interspersed with comedy sketches of drastically varying quality. Comedy duo Blair and Gary MacLean performed with Cummings, and even Bobby Hull joined in on the fun. It was a nostalgia tour, highlighting Cummings' Winnipeg roots. No filming actually took place *at* Portage and Main; the closest the special came were interstitial shots of Cummings and bandmates standing on concrete barricades outside of 201 Portage Avenue.

Reviews on the program were mixed. Randal McIlroy, a critic with the *Winnipeg Free Press*, wrote that while the music was good, he felt the overall show "was such a slick, smug essay of self-promotion and the dangers of the same."[272]

For another former member of the Guess Who, Randy Bachman, Portage and Main was more front and centre in one of his creative projects: the song "Prairie Town," which he performed in 1992 alongside another Winnipeg musician: Neil Young.

Like many other Winnipeg residents, Bachman had often taken the bus through the intersection growing up—past a large Coca-Cola sign on the Richardsons' lot, which displayed the time and temperature of the day. Bachman had moved out of Winnipeg in 1972 but sat down twenty years later to write a song about his former home city. "So when I wrote 'Prairie Town,'' says Bachman in his book *Randy Bachman's Vinyl Tap Stories*, "I remembered that sign and put in the line, 'Portage and Main, fifty below'."[273]

Neil Young's involvement in the song came after it was written. Bachman had sent the lyrics to Young's guitar tech, who showed it to Young, who then called up Bachman and asked to perform the song. So off Bachman went to Young's ranch, where two versions of the song were recorded. Young, too, had a personal connection to Winnipeg, having attended school in Winnipeg as a teen and starting his musical career playing in a variety of local bands.[274] Portage and Main, and Winnipeg as a whole, had some emotional significance for the both of them.

The concourse, too, has made an appearance in at least one song. Though not mentioned by name, The Weakerthans reference the underground in their love-hate Winnipeg anthem "One Great City": "Late afternoon, another day is nearly done/A darker grey is breaking through a lighter one/A thousand sharpened elbows in the underground/That hollow, hurried sound."

Portage and Main, 50 Below

When it comes to the harsh climate, Winnipeggers, in the words of historian James Gray, are "amiable braggarts."[275] This is a city that loves to talk about the weather, good or bad, always with the threat of a colder or rainier day around the corner.

Portage and Main has maintained a strong hold on being the hot spot for the worst of Winnipeg's weather. It is the coldest intersection in the city, or the windiest, or both. Some stretch the tale further. Maybe Portage and Main is the coldest spot in the country, or even the world.

Such stories have been a staple of the intersection for decades, though few were regularly put to print until the 1940s. In 1945, Private Arthur Madigan was photographed outside the Bank of Montreal at "what some call the 'coldest corner in the world,'" giving us some clue as to how long this had been a rumour.[276]

Around this same time, though, James Gray had mentioned that Winnipeg residents of 1947 could list colder, windier spots in the city. A joke contribution to the *Winnipeg Free Press* from 1926 alluded to the same thing:

> "And the Other One, Too, Of Course"
>
> Dear As You Like it, - After many years of careful and scientific investigation we find that the coldest corner in Winnipeg is
>
> The corner of Higgins and Main
>
> The corner of Portage and Main
>
> The corner of Donald and Main
>
> Etc.[277]

And Montreal reporter Frank Lowe, to "breach the gay sense of superiority these westerners seem to enjoy," argued that Montreal's Sun Life corner was colder and windier than Portage and Main.[278]

That it was cold and windy at Portage and Main, no one would deny. Some, however, set out to prove it was a bearable cold. *Winnipeg Tribune* reporter Leon Kossar took to the intersection in January of 1954, clad in only an old-fashioned bathing suit, to prove that "this business of weather…is all in the mind—whether you are in a buffalo coat today or in a bathing suit."[279]

Leon Kossar standing at Portage and Main in January
Winnipeg Tribune January 20, 1954 Winnipeg Tribune Archives/University of Manitoba

These stories had reached such a height by the 1960s that people set about studying them officially. Bill Bell, a researcher with the University of Winnipeg, gathered weather data in the greater Winnipeg area including its famous intersection in 1967. His goal was to map the temperature distribution across Winnipeg, and then factor in other details including wind speed, humidity, and cloud cover. At the end of the project, Bell hoped to be able to create a pollution model for the city to use. After three years of research, Bell questioned the idea that Portage and Main was the coldest area in Winnipeg. Cities act as heat islands, absorbing more heat through the grey and black concrete and warming the area through other emissions. Portage and Main, which saw heavy amounts of vehicle traffic and was surrounded by black and grey streets and similarly covered buildings, should hypothetically feel warmer. The issue at the corner was *not* the temperature, but the wind.

Wind chill factors were a relatively new concept in 1971. Environment Canada would only start using them in 1975. In 1971, reporters Val Werier and Jan Kamienski took it upon themselves to perform unofficial wind speed tests around the city.

The duo took to downtown Winnipeg: Werier with a notepad and Kamiesnki with a wind measuring device. It was January, with the weather office measuring the wind moving at six miles an hour. Winnipeg's weather office was measuring windspeeds at the airport, where there were fewer buildings to act as windbreaks.

Along the way, Kamienski started getting worried looks from pedestrians—the weather measuring set was an 18-inch aluminium rod, with a speed transmitter and direction vane, and from a distance looked something like an unusual weapon. At both Fort and Garry Street, they found the wind moving slower than the weather office had said. At Portage and Main, they found the wind travelling at four knots. Higher than the other corners, but slower than the recorded wind speed of the day.

To confirm their findings, Werier and Kamienski set out again on a day with faster winds. Their results were more or less the same. While the wind speed in downtown Winnipeg was lower than it was at the airport, the winds at Portage and Main were "twice as strong where they were funneled around the Richardson building. On that basis, a wind of 20 miles an hour elsewhere on Portage could be roaring at 40 miles around the Richardson building, as anyone could readily believe on a blustery day."[280]

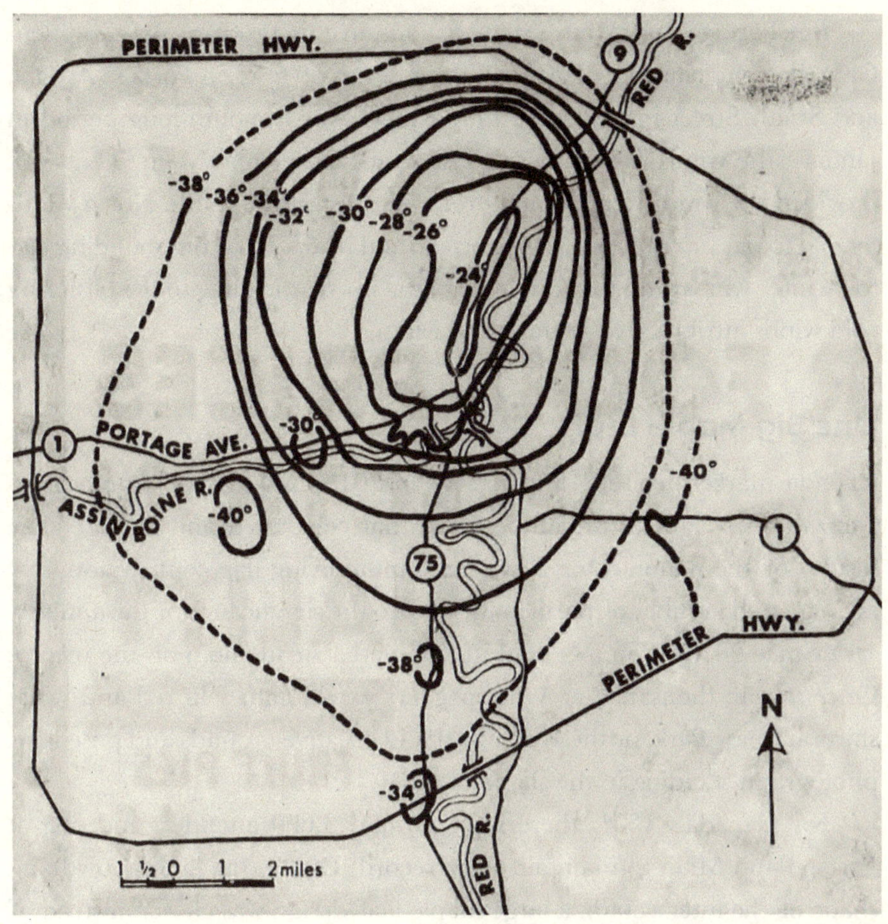

Bill Bell's geothermal map of Winnipeg
Winnipeg Tribune, February 25, 1970 Winnipeg Tribune Archives/University of Manitoba

A professor of architecture at the University of Manitoba, John D. Welch, observed that the architecture of Portage Avenue specifically allowed the winds to pick up such high speeds. Welch, alongside some intrepid students, set about measuring wind speeds in 1986 in order to better address urban design issues. In their findings, the wind at the Richardson Building could sometimes be registered at speeds of 43.2% higher than at the airport.

But Portage and Main was not alone in this problem. Environment Canada technician Bob Tortorelli ran a series of tests on Portage Avenue and Smith Street in 1980 and found that, over a month-long period in January, the winds were about as fast as at Portage and Main. That was, provided the winds were coming from the west or the south. North winds tended to pick up more speed at Portage and Main. As a compounding factor, winter winds tend to move in from the north—leading to the blistering cold winds attributed to Portage and Main.

One Big Maple Leaf

Canada marked its 150th anniversary in 2018, and across Winnipeg organizations sought to organize events that celebrated and explored the history of the nation. One event, an annual living flag competition, saw an increased number of participants due to the significance of the anniversary. Since 2013, Winnipeg had maintained a steady hold on the record. Once a year, thousands of Winnipeggers would gather in red and white shirts at Shaw Park, or the Forks, or the Legislative grounds and pose for a photograph standing in the shape of a flag.

For Canada's 150th, there were around 3,600 attendees meeting at Portage and Main to maintain their record. Due to the large crowd and shape of the intersection, a large maple leaf design was chosen instead of the much larger flag. Robert-Falcon Ouellette, Winnipeg Centre MP, and Mayor Brian Bowman both made speeches. The tone of the day was one of hope, of patriotism, and of a shared multicultural Canada.

But there were cracks in that image. Jagmeet Singh, NDP leader, was open about the difficulties surrounding Canada Day: "Part of that is remembering that this day is a difficult anniversary for Indigenous Peoples in Canada, as it is a celebration of the formal displacement of the first people of this land. We cannot mark this day without a solemn and respectful acknowledgement of our history, if we are to truly move towards reconciliation and justice."[281]

Protests

Portage and Main's reputation as a place for patriotic demonstrations, civic celebrations, and sporting victories have also made it an ideal location to go to challenge existing social norms. Gatherings at the intersection have not been limited to moments of joy. There have been protests and demonstrations at the corner, before and after the closing. These have come about as planned political action in response to contemporary concerns and as more spontaneous displays of collective anxiety, grief, and anger.

Post-war anxieties were evident in the type of displays happening at the corner following the 1950s. There was a 1962 march for nuclear disarmament which ran from the perimeter highway to the Legislature. It was a nine-mile walk meant to represent the area that would be destroyed should a 10-megaton bomb be dropped on Portage and Main. Similar Ban the Bomb walks took place simultaneously in Britain, the United States, and other Canadian cities.

Another group in favour of disarmament, the Canadian Voice of Women for Peace, staged regular demonstrations at the intersection throughout the 1960s. The group, which still exists today, was founded in 1960 in response to the Vietnam War and Cold War. The Manitoba chapter has been organizing speakers' events, debates, and demonstrations

A rainy 1962 silent vigil Portage and Main
Winnipeg Tribune Photo Collection, University of Manitoba Archives

since 1961. Among the roster of activities were silent vigils at Portage and Main, held near the War Monument outside the Bank of Montreal from 1962-1967.

The symbolism of it was obvious, even if it was not particularly liked. G.E. Hopkins, writing to the *Free Press*, called the choice "little less than sacrilege." It is impossible to get a sense of the individual members' perspectives on the matter, but we can get a small glimpse from a 1962 planning meeting. When organizing a Remembrance Day vigil, applause broke out after one group member volunteered support only if "we were not honoring the dead, but protecting the future."

Longer vigils were held annually on Mother's Day weekend, lasting a total of 24 hours (though members took shifts). There were two hundred women gathered for a miserable 1962 vigil, where the last five hours were spent standing in pouring rain. One member, Elizabeth Green, was eighty-seven years old and had agreed to spend two evenings at the vigil—even attempting to stay in the downpour despite the concern of her children. She had chosen the later shift specifically to avoid being photographed. In her own words: "I'm not doing it for publicity; I'm doing it with my whole heart."

These vigils remained a tradition until 1967, despite hecklers and bad weather. After that point, though, Voices of Women opted to set up a booth at the Red River Exhibition.

Idle No More

In the decades since, marches have been organized by student groups and activist organizations supporting peace movements, climate change policies, and Indigenous rights movements. In 1990, at the height of the Kanesatake Resistance in Quebec, Indigenous organizers in Manitoba set up a Peace Village at the grounds of the Legislature in solidarity with the Kanesatake First Nation. A September march, following the dismantling of the Peace Village, took the group of demonstrators past Portage and

Main. Out of this movement would come the federal government's Royal Commission on Aboriginal Peoples (1991), which concluded that relations between settlers and Indigenous nations needed to be restructured. The report provided a variety of means to do so, but lack of political will meant it was never properly implemented. Nearly twenty-three years later, the Idle No More movement began in Canada in response to yet another legislative decision. A new Canadian bill had been proposed, C-45, which would majorly restructure a number of important Canadian laws. This included the Indian Act, Navigable Waters Protection Act, and the Environmental Assessment Act—all of which threatened Indigenous sovereignty and important environmental protections in favour of expedited industrial developments.

Idle No More protestors at Portage and Main on December 31st, 2012
John Woods/Winnipeg Free Press

An open letter opposing the bill was signed by a number of Indigenous and environmental organizations and supported by nearly half a million Canadians. Locally, around four hundred people organized a rally at Portage and Main on December 31, 2012, to support the movement. It was a cold afternoon, sitting in the negative twenties with temperature made worse by Portage and Main's wind. Some braved the weather in traditional regalia, while others bundled up in coats and toques. Portage and Main had been deliberately chosen. According to event organizer Rhonda Head, "what better place to make a big statement than a busy intersection in Winnipeg to get the word out?"

After half an hour, the group moved north on Main towards Thunderbird House—but the brief event left a big impression. In a *Winnipeg Free Press* poll, only 21% of 13,422 respondents agreed both with Idle No More and the decision to block Portage and Main. Another 11% supported the movement, but not the gathering. At 46%, the largest block of respondents did not agree with Idle No More at all.

A certain amount of dissonance has always come with discussions regarding blocking traffic at Portage and Main. It has been allowed, even celebrated, for sports victories, block parties, and patriotic displays. Events which critique Canada's social fabric have not been given this same grace. Racism underscores nearly every conversation on the topic—rarely said outright, but clearly present.

It would almost seem as if the ideal protest should be held nearly out of sight, contained on sidewalks, or held near government buildings, kept away for the convenience of everyone else. But these protests being in public and being inconvenient were the point. In that same *Free Press* poll, another 22% admitted to not knowing much about the Idle No More movement at all. Indigenous and settler activists alike had been campaigning for the rights of Indigenous peoples for decades prior to 2012; this was not a new cause for those paying attention.

For those who weren't, it was often easy to turn a blind eye. And as a result, conditions worsened. The Idle No More movement was one of many tipping points, one which "changed the conversation between Indigenous and non-Indigenous peoples in this country. It demonstrated the capability, power, and savvy of Indigenous communities, and how Canada's theft of lands, systemic oppression and denial of treaty and Indigenous rights could not continue unabated."[282]

The Canadian government had stolen lands, languages, and culture from Indigenous communities. Highly visible protests, *inconvenient ones*, made this fact of our shared history harder to ignore. Idle No More would continue to hold demonstrations at Portage and Main in the following years, even after Prime Minister Stephen Harper met with delegates from the Assembly of First Nations in 2013. The group continues to act, supporting Indigenous rights movements and rallies and advocating for environmental protections across Canada.

And since that first Idle No More march, Portage and Main has become an important spot for Indigenous activists. New Year's Eve round dances took place for several years in a row across the 2010s. Then, in 2015, the National Inquiry into Missing and Murdered Indigenous Women and Girls confirmed what so many within their communities already knew. Studies found that the rate of homicide of Indigenous women was almost six times higher than non-Indigenous women. A 2004 Amnesty International report *No More Stolen Sisters* had identified this as a human rights crisis nearly a decade before. After decades of government inaction, attention was finally being paid to the issue. Idle No More's annual round dances at Portage and Main thus became centred around the topic, intensified after the discovery of sixteen-year-old Tina Fontaine's body at the Alexander Docks in 2016.

Despite the Calls to Action set forth by the Truth and Reconciliation Commission and the tireless work of activists, broader public apathy (or, in some cases, hostility) has led to slow progress. In 2022, the murders of four Indigenous women, Rebecca Contois, Morgan Harris, Marcedes

Myran, and Ashlee Shingoose, by serial killer Jeremy Skibicki sent shockwaves across not just Winnipeg, but Canada. So, too, did the provincial government's refusal to search Prairie Green Landfill and Brady Landfill for the women's remains.

The matter was still being debated when Linda Beardy's body was discovered at the Brady Road Landfill in April 2023. Her death had been accidental, the result of a tragic series of systemic failures, but it brought to mind the events of the past year.

Around five hundred people took to Portage and Main in a mass display of grief and sympathy. Beardy's family, both immediate and extended, led the march together. At Portage and Main, participants formed drum circles and sang and danced to honour the memories of Beardy, Contois, Harris, Myran, and Shingoose and to provide comfort to their grief-stricken families. Gerry Shingoose, one of the elders who helped organize the march, was candid about the circumstances that had led to Beardy's death. "We're sacred," Shingoose told reporters. "We're not trash."[283]

In 2024, Skibicki was found guilty on four counts of first-degree murder. Outside of the courthouse, the women's family members gathered with supporters and the general public around sacred fires. The end of a continually traumatizing investigation and the subsequent court case was a small relief, as was the guilty verdict. A smaller group left the courthouse for Portage and Main, where this time a round dance was held in celebration. And, in 2025, a humanitarian search of Prairie Green Landfill recovered the bodies of Harris and Myran, both from Long Plain First Nation, and returned them to the care of their families.

For much of its history, Portage and Main has represented the interests and identity of the establishment. Broadly Anglo-Saxon, broadly wealthy, and relatively new in the history of this continent. Idle No More's first demonstration at the corner, and all the ones that follow, are a needed reminder that Winnipeg's history runs much deeper than what is reflected at Portage and Main.

A round dance at Portage and Main in 2024, for International Women's Day
Ruth Bonneville/Winnipeg Free Press

Closing Portage and Main in 1979 had stopped regular pedestrian traffic, but it had not done much to stop people from rushing to the intersection for collective experiences. In fact, likely, the illicit nature of the gatherings made it all the more notable. Our tall tales about the weather, the nostalgic references to it in song, and the fact that Winnipeg's highs and lows have been commemorated at Portage and Main have cemented the intersection as something core to our identity. The reality of the space, though, has been underwhelming—though not for a lack of trying.

Chapter 9
To Open or Not To Open

"We don't know what to do with it," architect Wins Bridgman told the *Free Press* in 2003—referring, of course, to Portage and Main. "If we had a simple solution, we wouldn't need a competition. We're at an impasse, a 25-year impasse." [284]Bridgman was acting as professional advisor and coordinator for the City Crossing Design Competition, launched by Mayor Glen Murray in December of that year. Murray, for his part, referred to Portage and Main as "the traffic equivalent of a boarded-up building."[285]

If Bridgman's words seem dire, his take on it twenty years later gives things a more positive spin: "When something matters and we don't know what to do with it, that's a huge opportunity."[286] The City Crossing Design Competition was aimed at grasping that opportunity. It would last five months, with the ultimate goal of creating a new vision for Portage and Main.

Anyone could enter, so long as they had a licensed architect on their team, and each team had a hypothetical $10 million budget upon which to base their design. A prize of $100,000 would be divided amongst the winning teams.[287]

The challenges faced by designers, however, were complex. The design principles laid out included:

- Preserving and enhancing the city's treescape
- Mitigating wind

- Recognition of heritage
- Creating "a centre for pedestrian movement that is open, bright, accessible"
- Enriching the city with new public art
- Ensuring safety, both real and perceived
- Balancing the needs of pedestrians with traffic
- Implementing universal design for people with different abilities[288]

Moreover, City Crossing wasn't exactly an architectural competition in the traditional sense—it was an ideas competition, as Bridgman explained, and the hypothetical $10 million budget didn't really exist yet. He wasn't sure if the winning project would really get off the ground, but at minimum they could get a conversation started. At the same time, Bridgman said, they were "deadly serious."[289] The judges included urban designers and academics who would vet the winning entry, ideally so that it could eventually be constructed.

There was a slight hitch. As the competition's website explained, "Five separate private corporations plus the City of Winnipeg are landowners at Portage and Main. Portage and Main contains the mostly highly valued real estate in the City of Winnipeg. While all the separate corporations agree in the need for the site development, there is not, at this point, an agreement about the nature of redevelopment."[290]

More specifically, the sticking point was on the question of pedestrian crossings. While the competition would not disqualify entries calling for the opening of the intersection to foot traffic, the fine print acknowledged that "legal agreements between the City and property owners currently restrict pedestrian crossing at grade at Portage and Main."[6]

Over the course of the competition Bridgman often wrote poetically and inspiringly about Portage and Main. In January 2004, he wrote that "To reclaim Portage and Main is not to gaze nostalgically at the past. Its redevelopment can represent in our time a new balance between place and journey, public life and privatized travel."[291] This has been the theme of discussions around Portage and Main over the last two decades, it seems: a hopeful ambition paired with an undeniable frustration about the current state of the intersection.

Entries ran the gamut from functional to aesthetic, minimal to extravagant. Many used trees to beautify the intersection and to block the wind. Some suggested roundabouts, glass atriums, or above-ground walkways to extend the skywalk—creative solutions to the pedestrian problem. A number of designs proposed large architectural features at the intersection, including a large glass maple leaf and a huge, multi-coloured windmill. (This was not the first time an eye-catching feature was proposed for Winnipeg. In the 1990s Mayor Susan Thompson had proposed a laser pyramid above the city but never got the idea past city council's executive policy committee.)

Not all entries opened the intersection to pedestrians, but those that did not focused on making the concourse feel more open and on minimizing the transition from street level with skylights, gently sloping staircases, and glass atriums at the entrances. Some suggested making use of the then-new technology of digital screens to brighten the ambiance of the concourse.

The most out-there entry is the satirical "Republic of Portage and Main," which posed the question: "Is Portage & Main about myth, not place? Do we design the myth, not the place?" The team then presented the issue at hand: "Myths rely on collective engagement; Portage and Main has barricaded itself away; The myth is dying." Having considered this problem, Cohlmeyer Architects Ltd set about designing a new myth, rather than a new aesthetic design, for the intersection.[292]

Per their plan, the public would be the ones to enact the redesign—by force. Winnipeggers would storm the intersection with shovels and sledgehammers, removing the barriers and establishing the new "Republic of Portage and Main." Bits of rubble would be placed at the borders of this new republic, which would serve as a centre for a series of activities:

Light Forest, the winning design of the City Crossing Competition, envisioned trees at Portage and Main as well as tall light poles
Janet Rosenberg & Studio and Corbett Cibinel Architects

"street sports; drinking in the street; smoking zone; nude sunbathing (urban beach); impromptu film projections; skateboarding; building scaling; flea market; free coffee zone; cruising night; tomato throwing; bison run; day hotels… These activities, in conjunction with the development of Portage and Main, are like the gravity of a Black Hole—attracting passing photons; sometimes to slightly alter their trajectory, and sometimes to pull them irresistibly to the centre."[293]

The Republic of Portage and Main was firmly aimed at those who would keep pedestrians out of the intersection and contained some kernels of real advice and predictions: with pedestrians allowed in the intersection, "a new equilibrium" would emerge between cars and pedestrians. Businesses would benefit from the increased foot traffic.[294] The shutting out of people from Portage and Main had to go, in essence.

Aside from this tongue-in-cheek entry, the design teams who sent submissions to City Crossing took it extremely seriously. Bridgman emphasized the generosity of the architects and designers who worked on these projects: they spent their time and money on envisioning a better Winnipeg with no promise of anything in return.[295]

Light Forest

The winning entry of the City Crossing competition was called "Light Forest," submitted by Toronto landscape architecture firm Janet Rosenberg and Winnipeg firm Corbett Cibinel. Light Forest landed somewhere between practical and aesthetic, a "buildable concept." The team behind Light Forest took the term "crossing" and considered it: the crossing of the roads, of the Red and Assiniboine Rivers, of Indigenous and settler cultures. "Personally, I think that what we do wrong in Winnipeg is that really desperately would love to be Toronto and Vancouver and Chicago," said Doug Corbett, one of the designers behind Light Forest. Instead, they found unique inspiration in the tree-lined riverbanks of Winnipeg.[296]

Their design proposed the "reforestation of [Winnipeg's] downtown," both literally and in a more conceptual sense. Trees—real ones—would be planted on the boulevards and public spaces throughout downtown and leading to Portage and Main, where residents would encounter a forest made of lights. "High-tech polymer tubes" resembling huge light sabers, lit in various colours and rising from the ground and descending beneath, would connect the concourse and the street.[297]

The pedestrian problem would be solved simply with crosswalks set slightly back from the actual intersection. As a safety measure, medians would be added—a place for pedestrians to pause as they crossed. And on these would be "turbees"—small, urban windmills sourced from Denmark which would power the light tubes.

The original Light Forest design would have placed glass silos at the entryways, brightening the path to the concourse.
Janet Rosenberg & Studio and Corbett Cibinel Architects

They envisioned beautifying the concourse as well: widening the passages, adding skylights and other lighting sources. The dank stairways leading down—one of the most unappealing aspects of the concourse[298] would be replaced by large glass silos.

Winnipeg can feel like a harsh place sometimes: it is windy and cold for much of the year, buggy and hot the rest. The barricades are only part of the reason that Portage and Main leaves many Winnipeggers feeling alienated. While the nearby Exchange District brings some charm to downtown with its Chicago-esque brick architecture, most of the buildings at Portage and Main have sharp corners and rise high above the intersection. Light Forest aimed to "soften" the corner, to connect it to the rest of downtown, to the rivers, and ultimately to visitors.[299]

Less than a month after the announcement of the winner, however, a wrench was thrown in the works: Glen Murray resigned as mayor to run for federal office. Having lost its champion, the project lost some of its energy. "It went through the whims of politics," as Corbett put it.[300]

Murray's successor, Sam Katz, had publicly denounced the entire endeavor as a waste of time and money: "Why have a design competition unless you know you have the ability to accomplish your goal?"[301] Katz was referring to the agreement that still existed between the city and the property owners at Portage and Main, preventing the barriers from being removed. "A deal is a deal, and I can't change it," he said.[302] Katz would also, soon thereafter, cancel Murray's plans for a rapid transit line to the University of Manitoba.

Winnipeg had, evidently, exited its period of ambitious improvements and returned to a humbler status quo. Reactions to this shift were mixed. One letter to the *Free Press* called Katz "as close minded as the barricades are," while another thanked him "for rightfully casting aside your predecessor's fixation with bright shiny things."[303] Gord Steeves, Public Works Committee Chairman at the time and later a mayoral candidate, said "I am starting to get the feeling the Portage and Main issue is receding into the background and we aren't going to see it. It might not be revisited in the short term."[304]

Oddly, however, Katz had not completely shut down the project. Even while Katz was calling the project dead, Corbett was still engaged by the city to work on it: "I haven't been told to stop and I'll keep working until someone tells me otherwise," he told the *Free Press*.[305] And ironically, the project won an award of excellence from the Canadian Society of Landscape Architects in February 2005.[306]

In March, Katz sent a letter to the major landowners of Portage and Main asking each to contribute $11,500 towards a study of the design, while the city would contribute $69,500. Things were moving forward, it seemed, but Katz was still reticent: "I'm happy to listen. I don't believe anyone's going to be taking a sledgehammer to it soon."[307] Oxford Properties, who owned Winnipeg Square and had historically been the main opponent to any reopening plans, refused to comment to the *Free Press*.[308]

By June, however, a tentative agreement had been reached: the property owners would work with the city and with the designers of Light Forest to "determine which aspects of the design are acceptable, how much the changes would cost, who will pay for it, and when it will be built."[309] The designers had until the end of the year, about six months, to present a redesign.

A feasibility study completed in Summer of 2006 presented an altered plan: the polymer tubes would stay, but the ambitious plans for the concourse were dialed back. The glass silos were replaced with canoe-shaped shelters above some entrances, again inspired by the rivers, and the widening of the below-ground passages was nixed altogether for budget reasons. Most interestingly, the revised plan included an unusual compromise on the matter of pedestrian crossings. The concrete barricades would be removed, replaced instead with metal balustrades and timed gates. On weekends and after 5:20 p.m. on weekdays, the gates would open, allowing pedestrians to cross.[310]

By January 2007, six of seven property owners at Portage and Main had agreed to reopening the intersection with new timed gates. The plans seemed, once again, to have been dialed back, but would include lights and beautification efforts on a smaller scale. The lone holdout, once again, was Oxford Properties Group. *Free Press* journalist Bartley Kives pointed out the absurdity of keeping the intersection closed to bolster underground businesses that weren't even open outside of business hours: "On evenings and weekends, a small McDonald's counter is the only thing open in Winnipeg Square."[311]

Corbett remembered the last meeting he was at happening around June of 2006. "There was nothing definite. Nobody came and said, stop this tomfoolery or something like that, we're not going ahead. I think it might have just got down to everybody got a bit worn out."[312] Nobody seems to know exactly when the project ended, though the reason it ended is fairly evident: the Oxford Group would not budge, and Katz was not prepared to push them.

Winnipeg Square, deserted mid-day on a Saturday in 2025
Alex Judge

The Plebiscite

In 2014, incumbent mayoral candidate Brian Bowman announced his intention to open Portage and Main via Twitter: "Like City Hall, Portage & Main has been closed off to Wpger for too long. If elected mayor I pledge to re-open barriers to pedestrians."[313]

The promise was divisive. His opponent, Jenny Motkaluk, called the reopening a "vanity project" for Bowman, accusing him of throwing money intended for road repairs at "consultants and engineers who are going to make traffic worse at one of our busiest intersections."[314] Bowman was even at odds with his own public works director, who claimed a reopening would take two years—much longer than Bowman's proposed reopening plan.[315]

Nevertheless, Bowman spent the next few years attempting to build support for the idea. In 2016, Bowman took several mayors of other cities on a tour of the intersection. Calgary Mayor Naheed Nenshi, apparently, got "1,000 per cent lost" in the concourse—a common experience for Winnipeg tourists, no doubt.[316] In October 2017, Bowman posted to Twit-

The Bruce Head sculpture in the concourse, showing water damage
Alex Judge

ter: "If it ain't broken don't fix it, right? 40 yrs of infrastructure neglect at & under Portage&Main. Renewal is needed!"[317] His post was accompanied by four pictures showing mold, cracks, leaks, and other disrepair at the intersection. "Portage & Main needs to move beyond 1979," he wrote in another post.[318]

By 2018, however, Bowman had backed off a little. City councillor

Jeff Browaty pushed for the question to be put to the public through a referendum and eventually got all but one city councillor on his side. Even Bowman caved. The question, "Do you support the opening of Portage and Main to pedestrian crossings?" would be the first plebiscite question in thirty-five years put to Winnipeg voters.[319]

Browaty had put all his efforts into pushing against the reopening. In 2015, he was one of only two city councillors to vote against approaching property owners to revisit the issue (the other, incidentally, was current mayor Scott Gillingham).[320] Browaty called it a waste of money and resources and accused the mayor of "ramming through his plan" and hiding information from the public.[321] He made his message simple: "We need to stop this expensive, unnecessary plan."[322]

Free Press writer Dan Lett argued that Browaty was the one hiding information by pushing for a plebiscite when he knew Winnipeggers would not have all the relevant information: "Significant work, most of it performed above ground, will have to be done to restore or perhaps replace that membrane. Ironically, that work will likely require the removal of the pedestrian barriers that the 'no' forces fought so valiantly to save."[323] With this information not yet available, Browaty was able to emphasize the cost of the reopening—nearly $8 million, according to estimates at the time.

With the future of the intersection going to a vote, the debate around the issue heated up. A group of Winnipeggers formed Vote Open, a volunteer coalition aimed at supporting the opening of Portage and Main. Brent Bellamy, architect and creative director at Number Ten Architectural Group, became its de facto spokesperson—somewhat reticently, in his recollection—because he already had a public platform via his columns in the *Winnipeg Free Press.*

Bellamy talks about being struck many years ago by a mural depicting Portage and Main at the Canadian Museum of History: "It represented what a city should be ... and we just tossed it aside." For many decades now, Portage and Main has been little more than a thoroughfare—or an obstacle, if you're walking. Bellamy talks about "making it a place again."[324]

Vote Open tried to push the facts. The traffic delays would not be so bad, they said—about eighteen seconds on average.[325] Repairs needed to be done anyway, and the cost of reopening was a drop in the bucket compared to the overall city budget. They took flyers door to door and set up tables at that year's summer festivals and farmers' markets. Bellamy tried to get on TV and radio as much as possible. It was an uphill battle, though.

"It was completely unfair; it was destined to lose. The second it was proposed it was destined to lose." While Bellamy was forced to take time off from his *Free Press* column while he worked with Vote Open, city councillor Jeff Browaty was using his platform to its fullest extent to decry the idea of reopening. And it seemed that no other city councillor wanted to talk about it. Business leaders, too, had been scared off: Portage and Main had become a toxic subject.

More than a simple question of urban planning, one's position on Portage and Main had become a way of defining oneself. "No" voters were practical, no-nonsense folk who wanted their tax dollars going toward fixing potholes. "Yes" voters were cosmopolitan urbanists—yuppies, even. Depending on your social group, either position might carry a stigma. As a result, many local leaders were reluctant to tie themselves to one side or the other.

Asked why he got involved if Vote Open was destined to lose, Bellamy made a similar point to Wins Bridgman: it was about having a conversation, one that would make Winnipeggers ponder what a better Winnipeg could look like. Bridgman, incidentally, was still pushing for the reopening as well: in 2016, BridgmanCollaborative Architecture organized a Portage and Main crossing for Jane's Walk, an "annual festival of free, citizen-led walking conversations."[326] Led by Bridgman and by marketing director Marcella Poirier, around fifty pedestrians walked across the intersection, unphased by the drivers who honked and yelled.

Today, Brent Bellamy says he would approach the conversation differ-

Wins Bridgman and Marcella Poirier lead a group of pedestrians across Portage and Main in 2016.
Mike Deal / Winnipeg Free Press

ently: "I would flip it and really talk about what it could be as a place and sort of try to catch people's imaginations. Instead of trying to convince them that it won't be so bad, convince them that it's going to be awesome." Vote Open's more numbers-based approach was not working. A CBC-commissioned poll found that around two-thirds of Winnipeggers did not want to reopen Portage and Main to pedestrians: "There is no demographic—not young people, not downtowners, not downtown residents—who want to open the intersection. There is a broad and deep, intense dislike for this idea."[327]

The numbers showed, in fact, that support for reopening was at its lowest point in twenty years. Perhaps more significantly, Winnipeggers were both firmly entrenched and deeply annoyed about the debate. Seventy-six percent of respondents said they were "tired of hearing about Portage and Main." Around the same amount proclaimed that they were not open to changing their minds.[328]

The responses were not so clear-cut as they may seem, however, and in many ways, Winnipeggers contradicted themselves. Eighty-four percent of

Winnipeggers agreed that Portage and Main was an "important Winnipeg landmark," but 60% said they "don't really like spending time downtown." Only 31% saw it as a "critical issue for the city," but 48% said they "cared a great deal" about it.[329] It is also worth noting that the concerns of Winnipeggers were vastly different from the actual factors that had kept the intersection closed to this point. While the people of Winnipeg were concerned primarily with traffic flow, it was the business interests of Winnipeg Square in particular that had prevented a reopening to this point.

"I think most people felt that because they had never really experienced Portage and Main as a place. It has been, for almost 50 years, a place that we drive through—a place that we get angry that we're stuck in traffic," according to Brent Bellamy. Winnipeggers hadn't connected to Portage and Main on an emotional level in a long time, but they "did for many decades before that."

The results of the plebiscite were to be non-binding, but Bowman vowed to respect the wishes of the people: "If ultimately Winnipeggers are saying, 'Not yet, not now,' then we should respect that. At the end of the day, Winnipeggers and voters are always right."[330]

On October 24, 65% of Winnipeg voters elected to keep Portage and Main closed to pedestrians—to maintain the status quo.[331] Bowman, re-elected but with his pet project shot down, responded optimistically: "I don't think Portage and Main needs to be open for our downtown to succeed."[332]

Adam Dooley, a communications specialist and activist with Vote Open, expressed his disappointment but also the resilience of his side: "This issue isn't going away, and I don't think we'll be going away, either." His comments ended up being rather prescient: "At some point those barricades have to come down, when the intersection is repaired, and I think that there'll be an opportunity to continue discussion."[333]

A sky garden design proposed in a 2023 City of Winnipeg revitalization study
Rendering by HTFC, provided courtesy of the City of Winnipeg

A Survey Gone Wrong

Even in the immediate aftermath of the plebiscite, there were clues that the problem had not been put to bed. The city was still to spend some $2 million on repairs to the intersection, which "could result in the removal of some of the concrete barricades," the CBC reported in 2018. As it would turn out, $2 million was a highly optimistic estimate.[334]

Though there were no immediate changes following the citizen vote, decaying infrastructure, especially in the underground concourse, meant that while action on Portage and Main could be delayed, it could not be put off indefinitely.

In 2023, the city initiated a Portage and Main Revitalization Study and circulated an online survey looking for public input. The city also held stakeholder meetings and pop-up events. The study presented the public with several ideas that might be built in conjunction with the replacement of the waterproof membrane of the concourse.

The first set of ideas focused on the space above the intersection: a sky garden at sixth floor level described as a "raised plaza with plantings" where pedestrians could cross; a huge piece of public art, exact design to be determined; or a "raised garden ring" which would be aesthetic only and would not have public access. For the street edge, the designs presented showed lookout towers with viewing platforms or light poles with or without canopies. At the ground and building level, the designers offered up edge-to-edge paving, trees, and a vague notion of installing temporary public art.[335]

The results of the survey are not necessarily representative at a statistical level as respondents were self-selected, but with nearly 10,000 responses it certainly tells us something about how the mood in Winnipeg had shifted.

Asked what the city should keep in mind "when selecting the ideas that will go into the recommended vision for the intersection," respondents seemed to reject outright the ambitious designs that were being presented. Some 1,700 people simply demanded that the intersection be reopened. Suddenly, it seemed that the "Open" camp were the practical ones.

Respondents decried the use of public money for grand aesthetic designs that still kept pedestrians out. "Just open it to pedestrians. If you want vibrancy, you need people. Colossal, public dollars spent on these ridiculous monuments is not it," advised one respondent. Another, harsher response read: "Your idea of vision is nothing but art school doodling with a high price tag and all form over function. Time to grow up."

Many responses, if not most of them, also betray a certain exasperation: "I can't believe I'm reading another proposal for what to do with Portage and Main."

In response to the second open question about "what other kinds of activities, events, and features" respondents would like to see at the intersection, some gave genuine suggestions: outdoor sitting spaces, farmers' markets, festivals, and even a request for bagpipe music on special occasions. These responses were outweighed, however, by those who disregarded the question entirely and once again emphasized their desire to cross the street. What did they want? "Pedestrian crossings," "Being able to cross the street," "Walking. Literally the ability to cross the street."

One of the zanier ideas proposed in the 2023 revitalization study and survey: a set of lookout towers
Rendering by HTFC, provided courtesy of the City of Winnipeg

In 2018, Winnipeggers had not only voted "No" on pedestrian crossings, but they had also been firmly convinced that their minds would not be changed. What, then, was behind this shift in opinion? One response exemplifies the attitude of those who had switched sides: "I know when I voted against opening portage and main it was due to the cost. If we are spending money anyway then I would open portage and main."[336]

There are, of course, still many people who would prefer to see the intersection remain closed—around 40%, according to a 2024 poll.[337] But a swing from 33% support to 60% support in around six years is significant. In 2018, the activists with Vote Open found that people were unwilling to listen to the facts they presented. With several years to cool off from the height of the debate around the referendum, Winnipeggers were ready to consider the facts—and the costs in particular.

Brent Bellamy also feels that discussions have changed around urbanism. At city council, "The conversation is different now. They're talking about housing, they're talking about density."[338] One telling sign of this is how many respondents to the Revitalization survey specifically referenced Shibuya Crossing, a busy Tokyo intersection with scramble crossing. On

Reddit, in comment sections, among friends, Winnipeggers had evidently been talking about urban planning—how it's being done around the world, and how we can apply it at home. With citizens showing more engagement on this subject, conversations in city hall now regularly include discussions about housing and density.

"Folks, this is just an intersection."

Mayor Scott Gillingham has said this so many times that it's become a kind of a catchphrase. His staff even had it printed on a mug. Something about the way Gillingham has presented the issue seems to have resonated with Winnipeggers. "This is just an intersection": Gillingham presents it almost with a slight shrug, a "What can you do?"

In 2024, it was with this approach that Gillingham announced—after so many years of closure and nearly as many of debates—that Portage and Main would reopen to pedestrian traffic. Gillingham recognizes the historic and cultural significance of Portage and Main, but at the end of the day he is a practical man. And to some extent, there was no choice at all. Recent city estimates show that to replace the waterproof membrane protecting the concourse would cost $73 million— possibly more—and would cause four to five years of traffic delays.[339]

Gillingham has other reasons, too: for one, the pandemic has changed traffic flow patterns. Portage and Main is no longer the city's busiest intersection—nor has it been for some time.

At their core, Winnipeggers are deeply practical people. With the days of hotly debating the subject behind us, given time and space to consider, most people have found these arguments convincing.

So ultimately, the reopening will not be a grand vision—neither light forest nor a floating garden. It will be a straightforward intersection, barriers removed, open to pedestrians. An intersection like many others in our city. "I'm trying to manage expectations," Gillingham says. But there are

The vision approved by city council, providing a more realistic view of what Portage and Main might look like in the future
Rendering by HTFC, provided courtesy of the City of Winnipeg

opportunities in a blank slate. Wins Bridgman points out that the abandonment of downtown during the pandemic has led to a re-Indigenization: the MMF purchase of the Bank of Montreal, the redevelopment of the Hudson's Bay Building, and more. Bridgman says he is more optimistic about Winnipeg than he has ever been.[340]

Mayor Gillingham, too, says he has seen "a lot of reinvigoration and redevelopment happening on all four quadrants of our town." That reopening Portage and Main will connect all these new ventures: Marketlands, the Forks Railside, True North Square, and likely more to come. He envisions a future where Winnipeg feels more like it does on Nuit Blanche: with people milling around, after work hours, enjoying the city.[341]

The loss, of course, will be the concourse. It won't close immediately, but its remaining lifespan is unclear. And despite the very real problems of the concourse—the smelly entryways, the maze-like construction, the empty storefronts—it has served its purpose in protecting local residents and workers from Winnipeg's coldest days.

Perhaps this is the price of our indecision: had we developed Light

Forest, or indeed any vision, twenty years ago, maybe both a pedestrian crossing and a healthier concourse could have developed in tandem. Instead, we let run-down infrastructure make the decision for us. We let an icon—a space that has held so many of our most important stories from thousand-year-old trade routes, to class warfare, to hockey celebrations—become "just an intersection."

Epilogue:
The Meaning of an Intersection

What will it mean to cross Portage and Main for the first time? Will we feel the triumph of those who have fought to reopen it, or the spirit of the strikers and the unemployed who gathered there? Will we pause to see the view all the way down Portage before rushing to catch the light?

Likely the novelty will wear off quickly. We'll become used to crossing at street level, and cars and pedestrians will eventually find an easy balance as they do elsewhere in the city. It *is* just an intersection, after all.

But something about Portage and Main pulls us to it. It's where we go to shout: in joy, in anger, in despair.

Maybe it's just a matter of geography. Portage and Main is in the heart of downtown, a busy thoroughfare. Stepping onto the street there, disrupting the regular flow of traffic, is sure to make a statement.

Maybe it is the history of the place. Taking a protest to Portage and Main is a well-trodden path established by those before us.

In many ways, Portage and Main has belonged to those in power. Though the buildings and businesses at the intersection have changed many times over, they have nearly always been in the hands of wealthy individuals and corporations. Maybe it is this that draws us in. Here is a place where we can shout directly into the face of authority; here we cannot be ignored. By stepping into the intersection, we assert that this is our city, too.

For over a hundred years, various authorities have tried to keep Winnipeggers out of the intersection. Eventually, barriers and an underground mall did the trick—more or less. Is it not only special police and business interests who keep us out, however. In recent years, Winnipeggers themselves have rallied against the idea of people at Portage and Main.

And yet, this is not always so. Even those who voted against a reopening have sometimes found their way into the intersection for Whiteout Parties. But, if people are permitted to flock to Portage and Main in collective moments of celebration, shouldn't the same be true for moments of grief, of anger, of collective pain in response to social injustices? Through the intersection, we can see a microcosm of a much larger discussion: who is this city for?

This year, 2025, the mayor is placing a piece of the barricades into a time capsule, to be opened in fifty years. "Maybe it will mean a lot more to us than it will to them," he says. And maybe he's right.

Portage and Main has held a role in so many of our city's stories. It has seen the highs, lows, and odd in-betweens of Winnipeg's history. Maybe, in fifty years time, we will have created a place that more accurately reflects Winnipeg's strange beating heart.

Acknowledgements

Winnipeg's heritage community is small in the good way: tight-knit and supportive. We thank all the people who dedicate their time (paid, unpaid, and underpaid) to ensuring that Manitoba's history is told: archivists, authors, conservators, interns, and many more. We give special thanks to the Manitoba Historical Society for making Manitoba history so accessible.

Our work is made so much easier by the historians before us who have compiled the disparate pieces of the past into coherent narratives. In this respect we thank the late Jim Blanchard, whose books are invaluable. We wish he had had the time to write many more.

We also have to thank our producer and friend Nick Friesen, for his endless support. If you're reading this, go check out his other projects at Inservice Comics. We would also like to thank associate producers Samson and Phoebe (even if Samson bit Sabrina once or twice, but who's counting).

A *huge* thank you to the team at Great Plains Press, who have made publishing a book (a big scary endeavour) into something fun, and exciting, and only moderately daunting. Thank you to Mel, Angeline, and Catharina!

Finally, we do have to thank Winnipeg—a place whose weird, conflicting, and deeply frustrating history has shaped the trajectory of our careers.

Sabrina

So much of my life has been largely shaped by the many communities I have been lucky enough to be a part of. So, to that end, I have to thank my hometown of Morris, Manitoba and my family, friends, and teachers there. There is also the Faculty of History at the University of Winnipeg, and the History Students Association (where I would meet Alex, nearly ten years ago to the publication of this book), and the non-profit boards I have been a part of.

I have to thank my family, both immediate and extended, who have always accepted (and maybe sometimes just tolerated) my oddball interests. To my mom, for not batting an eyelash when I decided to become a history major with no broader career plans, and my siblings Adam and Kamryn for humbling me, at all times, whether I like it or not. To Andre, for everything.

To Nick—to all those years ago, when a week into working together, you came to my desk and asked, "Do you like podcasts?" Look how that turned out.

And, of course, to Alex. Thank you for being a friend.

Alex

I owe a lifetime of gratitude to the University of Winnipeg History Department and, especially, to the History Students Association. I was an isolated and nervous young adult when I arrived, and the university gave me a sense of community that I desperately needed.

There are so many professors who shaped my understanding of history and my enthusiasm for the past. Among them Dr. Paul Lawrie, who was my greatest mentor and with whom I had so many good talks. Dr. Eliakim Sibanda, who encouraged me to be an active participant in the world and who stepped in with a last-minute reference for grad school. Dr. Rick Halpern, who was the emotional cornerstone of my grad school experience and always reminded me to be excited about my work. And Dr.

Andriy Zayarnyuk, who taught one of the most rigorous classes I ever took and who pushed me to prove myself.

I also owe thanks to my dad and to my sisters Laina and Kira, all of whom have indulged many history lectures disguised as "fun facts." And my partner, who made potato pancakes and let me nap when I got too stressed out from researching.

And finally, to my co-host and co-author and good friend Sabrina, whose energy is infectious, and to friend and producer Nick, who always tells us how good our ideas are.

Endnotes

Chapter 1: Nestaweya and the Fur Trade

[1] Peguis's recollections were delivered orally to citizens of Red River in 1863, though a reporter for the *Nor'Wester* recorded and published it. "Important Statement of Pegowis Indian Chief" *The Nor'Wester*, October 14, 1863 (3)

[2] "Important Statement of Pegowis, The Indian Chief," *The Nor'wester*, October 14, 1863 (3)

[3] Ibid.

[4] Ibid.

Chapter 2: Creating an Intersection

[5] Taché, Alexandre-Antonin, "Sketch of the North-West of America," *The New Nation*, August 6, 1870 (1).

[6] As other historians have pointed out, "McKenney" is spelled in just about every possible way in contemporary materials, including: McKenny, McKinney, McKenna, McKenty, McKinnon, etc. We have chosen "McKenney" here for the sake of consistency.

[7] Hargrave, Joseph James *Red River* (Montreal: Printed by John Lovell, 1871). (200)

[8] Begg, Alexander *Red River Journal and other papers relative to the Red River Resistance of 1869-1870* (Toronto: Champlain Society, 1956). (296)

[9] Hargrave, *Red River.* (200)

[10] George F. Reynolds, "The Man Who Created the Corner of Portage and Main," *MHS Transaction* 3, no 26 (1969-70).

[11] Ronaghan, Neil Edgar "The Archibald Administration in Manitoba, 1870-1870" (PhD Dissertation: University of Manitoba, 1987). (15)

[12] Hargrave, *Red River* (307)

[13] Reynolds, *The Man*

[14] Hargrave, *Red River* (308)

[15] "Going Ahead," *The Nor'Wester,* October 22, 1862. (3)

[16] Bryce, George "The Illustrated History of Winnipeg," *Manitoba Free Press,* March 25, 1905. (17)

[17] District of Assiniboia General Quarterly Court, 1863-1872. Council of Assiniboia Fonds, P7538/3, Provincial Archives of Manitoba.

[18] "Our Future Capital," *The Nor'Wester*, April 13th, 1863. (2)

[19] District of Assiniboia, Provincial Archives of Manitoba

[20] District of Assiniboia, Provincial Archives of Manitoba

[21] Begg, *Red River Journal* (209)

[22] Sources differ as to whether George Emmerling built a second hotel (meaning that McKenney's original Royal Hotel would have been at a different spot) or whether he merely built an addition onto the Royal.

[23] While unproven, it is theorized that Larsen may have taken the iconic photograph of Louis Riel and his companions during the Red River Resistance.

[24] "A Shooting Affray," *Red River Pioneer* December 1, 1869. (2)

[25] "Robberies: Discovery of the Missing Property," *Manitoban and Northwest Herald*, April 29, 1871. (3) It appears Larsen was using his old Portage and Main Store to smuggle stolen goods, though like Larsen's other crimes, it never made it to trial.

[26] Craig, Irene "Grease Paint on the Prairies: An Account of the Theatres, the Plays, and the Players of Winnipeg from 1866 to 1921," *MHS Transactions* Series 3, April 1947.
[27] Hargrave, *Red River* (420)
[28] Begg & Nursey, *Ten Years in Winnipeg* (8)
[29] Hartman, James B. "The Churches of Early Winnipeg," *Manitoba History* 45 (Spring/Summer 2003).
[30] Ibid.
[31] Garrioch, Rev. A.C. First Furrows: *A History of the Early Settlement of the Red River Country, including that of Portage la Prairie* (Winnipeg: Stovel Company Limited, 1923). (171)
[32] Begg & Nursey, *Ten Years in Winnipeg* (12)
[33] Goldsborough, Gordon and Nathan Kramer, "Winnipeg Board of Trade/Winnipeg Chamber of Commerce," *Manitoba Historical Society*, revised March 18, 2025.
[34] Hall, Frank "Oh Be Joyful," *Manitoba Pageant* 22, no. 2 (Winter 1977).
[35] "City's Old Timer A Western M.P.P.," *Manitoba Free Press*, March 22, 1907. (5)
[36] "The Reign of Terror in Red River Parish and Vicinity," *New York Times*, September 15, 1874. (6)
[37] Many sources claim that Goulet was chased from the Red Saloon, at the corner of Portage and Main. However, the inquest into his death makes it clear that Montchamp was the proprietor of the saloon Goulet was in. This is also evidenced by the fact that Goulet ran down Post Office/Lombard, the quickest route to the river from Montchamp's (but not from the Red Saloon). The original source of this error may be uncareful readings of A.C.G. Garrioch's *First Furrows*, in which he discusses the Red Saloon "and other such drinking places" before turning to the death of Goulet without, however, specifying that the Red Saloon is where this actually happened.
[38] George Reynolds has pointed out that this rumour, propagated by Alexander Begg, may have been caused by McKenney's unpopular political position.
[39] Begg & Nursey, *Ten years in Winnipeg* (3)
[40] Bryce, George "Early Days in Winnipeg," *MHS Transactions* 1, no. 46 (February 1894).
[41] There has been some confusion as to whether it was McKenney's Portage and Main general store or his warehouse, just north of the store, that was rented for city council. Bruce Cherney did an excellent investigation into this for his historical column in the *Real Estate News*.

Chapter 3: An Intersection Takes Shape

[42] "The Incorporation of Our Town," *The Manitoba Trade Review*, Vol. 1, no. 1 (Jan. 1, 1872)
[43] "Residents of Ontario," *Manitoba Free Press*, 12 August 1875. (3)
[44] Healy, W.J. *Winnipeg's Early Days*, Winnipeg, 1927. (23)
[45] "Asked to Change it Once More," *Winnipeg Daily Sun*, January 12, 1884 (8)
[46] "A Petition," *Winnipeg Free Press*, January 4, 1884 (4)
[47] "Asked to Change it Once More," *Winnipeg Daily Sun*, January 12, 1884 (8)
[48] Bradley, Walter E. "A History of Transportation in Winnipeg." *Manitoba Transactions*, 1957/58.
[49] "New Nanton Block Affected by Rain Causes Anxiety," *Morning Telegram*, August 13, 1907. (1,11)
[50] "Experts here To Investigate," *Winnipeg Tribune*, August 19, 1907. (6)
[51] "Anthem in Steel Downs all Sound in the New Nanton Block" *Winnipeg Tribune*, July 24, 1909. (17)
[52] "Huge Heating Boiler," *Winnipeg Tribune*, December 29, 1909. (9)
[53] "Real Estate Men Are Kept Hustling," *Winnipeg Tribune*, September 25, 1909. (25)

[54] Begg & Nursey, *Ten Years in Winnipeg* (221)

[55] "Offered 320,000 for Queen's Hotel," *Winnipeg Tribune,* May 10, 1905 (10)

[56] "The Renovated Queen Hotel," *Winnipeg Free Press*, September 10, 1908 (2)

[57] "Nos hommes d'affaires Canadiens-Francais du Sacre-Couer de Winnipeg," *La Liberté* January 1, 1919. (8).

[58] "Donaldson's Corner" *Winnipeg Free Press*, February 10, 1883. (8)

[59] "The Handsomest Building in the City," *Winnipeg Evening Tribune*, February 21, 1910. (3)

[60] *Winnipeg Telegram*, January 24, 1914. (13)

Chapter 4: Growing Pains

[61] "Winnipeg's Ever Widening Circle of Millionaires," *Winnipeg Telegram*, January 29, 1910.

[62] Blanchard, Jim *Winnipeg 1912* (Winnipeg: University of Manitoba Press, 2005) (90)

[63] MacBeth, R.G. *Sir Augustus Nanton: A Biography* (Toronto: MacMillan, 1931). (16)

[64] Blanchard, *Winnipeg 1912.* (93)

[65] Blanchard, *Winnipeg 1912.* (253)

[66] Smith, Doug *Let Us Rise! An Illustrated History of the Manitoba Labour Movement* (Winnipeg: Public Press, 1985). (26)

[67] *The Voice*, "Wanted," July 7, 1916 (p.8).

[68] Street Cars Are Wrecked; Militia to Be Called Out," *Winnipeg Tribune*, March 29, 1906. (1)

[69] Ibid.

[70] "Street Railway Service Tied Up," *The Voice*, March 30, 1906. (1)

[71] "Street Cars Are Wrecked; Militia to Be Called Out," *Winnipeg Tribune*, March 29, 1906. (1)

[72] Johnson, A. Ernest, *The Strikes in Winnipeg in May 1918: The prelude to 1919?* Master's thesis (University of Manitoba, 1978), (63).

[73] Johnson, *The Strikes in Winnipeg. (*74)

[74] Johnson, *The Strikes in Winnipeg.* (86)

[75] Kramer, Reinhold and Tom Mitchell, *When the State Trembled* (Toronto: University of Toronto Press, 2010). (47-48)

[76] *The Voice*, May 17, 1918. (1)

[77] Summary of Strike Situation," *Winnipeg Evening Tribune*, May 16, 1918. (1)

[78] "The Strike Score Today," *Winnipeg Evening Tribune* May 21, 1918 (1)

[79] "50,000 Citizens Join Walk-out to Reach Offices," *Winnipeg Evening Tribune*, May 22, 1918.

[80] Ibid.

[81] Ibid

[82] Kramer and Mitchell, *When the State Trembled.* (49)

[83] Ibid.

[84] Smith, Doug, Let Us Rise. (36)

[85] Bercuson, David Jay, Confrontation at *Winnipeg: Labour, Industrial Relations, and the General Strike* (Montreal & Kingston: McGill-Queen's University Press, 1990). (116)

[86] David Thompson, "From Patriotism to Insurgency: The Shifting Allegiances of Winnipeg 1919's Striker-Soldiers," in *For a Better World: The Winnipeg General Strike & The Workers' Revolt,* ed. James Naylor, Rhonda L. Hinther, Jim Mochoruk (Winnipeg: University of Manitoba Press, 2022). (62)

[87] Bercuson, *Confrontation at Winnipeg*. (150)

[88] Mounted Policemen Charge Huge Crowd at Portage and Main," *Winnipeg Evening Tribune,*

"June 10, 1919. (1)
[89] "Strikers Throw Eggs at Police; Rioting Starts," *Winnipeg Telegram,* June 10, 1919. (1)
[90] "Police Kept Off Streets After Fighting," *Winnipeg Evening Tribune,* June 11, 1919. (2)
[91] Ibid.
[92] Ibid.
[93] Bercuson, *Confrontation.* (154)
[94] "Victoria cross hero attacked in street by Austrian thugs," *Winnipeg Evening Tribune*, June 11, 1919. (1)
[95] Ibid.
[96] "Sergeant Coppin Rallies Quickly From His Hurts," *Winnipeg Telegram Strike Editions*, June 11, 1919. (1)
[97] "Sergt. Coppins V.C., Narrowly Escaped Death at Hands of Aliens During Riot," *Manitoba Free Press,* June 11, 1919. (1)
[98] "A Significant Fact," *Western Labor News*, June 11, 1919. (3)
[99] "City Keeps Mounted Police Off Streets; 'Main Front' Quiet," *Winnipeg Evening Tribune,* June 11, 1919 (1).
[100] Bercuson, *Confrontation* (155)
[101] "Friction Was Local," *Manitoba Free Press*, February 15, 1919. (17)
[102] "Car Service to be Resumed Thursday, M'Limont Announces," *Winnipeg Evening Tribune,* June 10, 1919. (1)
[103] "Trolley Men To Stay Out," *Winnipeg Evening Tribune*, June 11, 1919. (1)
[104] Lewycky, Dennis *Magnificent Fight: The 1919 General Strike* (Halifax & Winnipeg: Fernwood Publishing, 2019). (44-45)
[105] Bercuson, *Confrontation*, p.174
[106] "Opening Day of Red Cross Drive Indicates Complete Success," *Manitoba Free Press*, April 10, 1918. (4); "Social and Personal," *Manitoba Free Press*, April 30, 1918. (8)
[107] MacBeth, *Sir Augustus Nanton* (45-46)
[108] Kramer and Mitchell, *When the State Trembled* (48)
[109] "High Prices and High Wages," *Western Labor News*, May 21, 1919. (4)
[110] "By Permission," *Western Labor News*, May 27, 1919. (4)
[111] "The Soldier and The Strike," *Western Labor News*, June 2, 1919. (3)
[112] Ibid.
[113] Lewycky, *Magnificent Fight* (19)
[114] Nanton, Paul, *Prairie Explosion: Setting the Pace for Canada* (Canada, Nanton Press, 2010). (126-127)
[115] Nanton, Paul "A.M. Nanton's 41 Years in Winnipeg, 1883-1924," *Manitoba History* 6 (Fall 1983).
[116] Ibid.
[117] MacBeth, *Sir Augustus Nanton.* (65)
[118] Blanchard, Jim, *Thinking Big: A History of the Winnipeg Business Community to the Second World War* (Winnipeg: Great Plains, 2021).
[119] Blanchard, Jim, *A Diminished Roar* (Winnipeg: University of Manitoba Press, 2019). (20)
[120] Levine, Allan *The Exchange: 100 Years of Trading Grain in Winnipeg* (Winnipeg: Peguis Publishers Limited, 1987). (106)
[121] Manitobans largely supported the temperance movement. In 1916, prohibition was enacted through a provincial referendum. For most of this period it was still legal to import liquor from

other provinces and consume it in private, making illegal speakeasies mostly unnecessary.
[122] "Cenotaph Dedicated to Glorious Dead," *Manitoba Free Press*, June 14, 1920. (3)
[123] "Montreal Bank Statue Unveiled," *Winnipeg Evening Tribune*, December 5, 1923 (3)
[124] Ibid.
[125] Ibid.
[126] "Judges Select Winning Design for Cenotaph," *Winnipeg Evening Tribun*e, December 23, 1925. (1)
[127] "Protest Against Cenotaph Design to be Reviewed by War Memorial Committee," *Winnipeg Evening Tribune* February 25, 1926. (9)
[128] Ibid.
[129] Ibid.
[130] Ibid.
[131] Winnipeg War Memorial Committee fonds, Archives of Manitoba
[132] Winnipeg War Memorial Committee fonds, Archives of Manitoba
[133] "Wife of Emanual Hahn, Canadian Born Girl, Wins Winnipeg
Cenotaph Award" *Winnipeg Evening Tribune*, November 12, 1927 (1)
[134] Ibid.
[135] "First Prize in Cenotaph Competition," *Manitoba Free Press*, November 12, 1927. (1)
[136] R.P., "The Cenotaph Design," *Winnipeg Evening Tribune*, November 11, 1927. (29)
[137] Harris, W. P. "Charges Bad Taste," *Winnipeg Evening Tribune*, December 10, 1927 (17)
[138] Mulock, W. Redford, "Re the Cenotaph," *Winnipeg Evening Tribune*, December 10, 1927 (17)
[139] Blanchard, *Diminished Roar* (260)
[140] "City all set for Jubilee; plans complete," *Winnipeg Evening Tribune*, June 17, 1924. (1)
[141] Winnipeg 50th anniversary scrapbook, 1924. City of Winnipeg Archives.
[142] Civic Social and Athletic Association, Winnipeg – Know Our City: *Souvenir of Winnipeg's Jubilee* 1874-1924 (Winnipeg: West Canada Publishing Co., 1924).
[143] "Daylight Caravan to Minneapolis Wins Race Against Sun," *Winnipeg Evening Tribune,* May 16,1925 (16)
[144] Ibid.
[145] "Daylight Dash a Triumph," *Winnipeg Evening Tribune* May 16, 1925. (1)

Chapter 5: The Depression

[146] Dettloff, C.P. "Here and There With the Camera," *Winnipeg Evening Tribune*, December 27, 1933. (3)
[147] "Real Estate Values in Downtown Winnipeg Have Multiplied by One Hundred in the Course of Forty Years," *Winnipeg Evening Tribune*, February 26, 1930. (47)
[148] Gray, James H., *The Winter Years*: The Depression on the Prairies (Calgary: Fifth House Ltd, 2003), 13.
[149] Goldsborough, Gordon, "MHS Centennial Business: James Richardson & Sons Limited / Pioneer Grain Company / Richardson Pioneer James Richardson & Sons," *Manitoba Historical Society*, revised January 11, 2025. https://www.mhs.mb.ca/docs/business/jamesrichardson.shtml
[150] "Skyscraper to be built at Portage, Main," *Winnipeg Evening Tribune*, July 19, 1929. (1)
[151] "New Richardson Building Holds Well Within City's Skyscraper Legislation," *Winnipeg Evening Tribune,* July 27,1929. (2).

[152] "Skyscraper to be built at Portage, Main," *Winnipeg Evening Tribune*, July 19, 1929. (1)
[153] Blanchard, *A Diminished Roar,* (265) "Skyscraper to be built at Portage, Main," *Winnipeg Evening Tribune* July 19, 1929. (1)
[154] "Skyscraper to be built at Portage, Main," *Winnipeg Evening Tribune*, July 19, 1929. (1)
[155] "Work May Start on Richardson Building Soon," *Winnipeg Evening Tribune*, October 2, 1929. (2)
[156] "Sign of Half Century Ago Is Uncovered," *Winnipeg Evening Tribune,* October 30, 1929. (4)
[157] "Stocks and Grain Crash in Near Panic," *Winnipeg Evening Tribune*, October 24, 1929. (1)
[158] "Stocks Recover; Market Chaos Ends," *Winnipeg Evening Tribune*, October 25, 1929. (1)
[159] Gray, *The Winter Years* (5)
[160] Gray, *The Winter Years* (3)
[161] "Permits Issued in Three Months Total $1,385,405," *Winnipeg Evening Tribune* March 29, 1930. (14)
[162] "Work on Richardson Building Suspended," *Winnipeg Evening Tribune*, November 19, 1929. (4)
[163] "Excavation for Richardson Bld. To Be Filled In," *Winnipeg Evening Tribune*, March 31, 1930. (3)
[164] "Big Square in Centre of City is Mayor's Aim," *Winnipeg Evening Tribune* May 5, 1930. (1)
[165] Ibid.
[166] "City's Finest Service Station at City's Busiest Corner," *Winnipeg Evening Tribune*, June 28, 1934. (5)
[167] Dettloff, C.P. "Here and There With The Camera," *Winnipeg Evening Tribune*, January 13, 1934. (3)
[168] Ibid.
[169] Canada General Statistics Branch, *The Canada Yearbook* 1934-35 (Ottawa: J.O. Patenaude, 1935). (738)
[170] Gray, *The Winter Years* (158)
[171] Ibid.
[172] "Mayor Webb's Casting Vote Decides Issue," *Winnipeg Evening Tribune*, May 27, 1930. (3)
[173] Anderson, Allan, "The Forgotten Man," *Winnipeg Evening Tribune*, October 30, 1934. (5)
[174] "Careless Pedestrians Require Education," *Winnipeg Evening Tribune*, October 30, 1934. (5)
[175], "Deputations Hold Parallel Parking Proved Unnecessary By Recent Traffic Census," May 23, (p.9).
[176] "City Will Again Try to Get Half of Gasoline Tax," *Winnipeg Evening Tribune*, March 3, 1931. (5)
[177] "Council Approves Plan to Charge Parked Motorists; Will Ask For Legislation," *Winnipeg Evening Tribune*, March 9, 1937. (1)
[178] "Man of 80 is knocked down by motor car," *Winnipeg Evening Tribune*, October 3, 1933. (2)
[179] "Eight injured over weekend in auto mishaps," *Winnipeg Evening Tribune,* September 5, 1933. (8)
[180] "Freak accident victim is only slightly injured," *Winnipeg Evening Tribune*, April 2, 1936. (2)
[181] "Game bird flies into street car; is unhurt, released," *Winnipeg Evening Tribune*, November 4, 1937. (4)
[182] Thompson, J.E. "Drivers Much To Blame For Jay-Walking Habit," *Winnipeg Evening Tribune*, June 2, 1938. (3-4)
[183] Ibid.
[184] Thompson, J.E. "Education Best Hope To Reduce Accidents," *Winnipeg Evening Tribune*, June

3, 1938. (3, 5)
[185] "Safe Driving Winners To Be Parade Feature," *Winnipeg Evening Tribune*," May 27, 1938. (3)
[186] "Twenty Traffic Control Signals Will Be Erected," *Winnipeg Evening Tribune*, September 30, 1930. (3)
[187] "Says Timing 'Absolutely Rotten,'" *Winnipeg Evening Tribune*, March 5, 1931. (8)
[188] "Pedestrians Made Safer," *Winnipeg Evening Tribune*, January 28, 1937. (13)
[189] Ruddell, S.G. "City-Owned Vacant Lots and Building Problem," *Winnipeg Evening Tribune*, November 20, 1937. (24)
[190] "Streets Will Be Decorated for Christmas," *Winnipeg Evening Tribun*e, December 9, 1930. (3)
[191] "Winnipeg to Extend Bilingual Welcome," *Winnipeg Tribune*, August 31, 1938. (4)
[192] "Biggest Easter Egg," *Winnipeg Evening Tribune*, March 27, 1937. (15)
[193] "Bunnell Also Suggests W.E. Taxes Be Cut," *Winnipeg Evening Tribune*, March 6, 1931. (1)
[194] "Rooms," *Winnipeg Evening Tribune*, July 3, 1934. (17)
[195] "Farm Lands," *Winnipeg Evening Tribune*, April 30, 1937. (26)
[196] "Poppy Day is Bringing Good City Response," *Winnipeg Evening Tribune*, November 10, 1933. (3)
[197] "Dogs turn out as taggers for Humane Society," *Winnipeg Evening Tribune*, June 20, 1936. (3)
[198] "Man Attempts to Steal Cash Box of Lady Tagger," *Winnipeg Evening Tribune*, June 13, 1931. (1)
[199] "Canadian Prosperity Weeks Starts on Saturday," *Winnipeg Evening Tribune*, October 10, 1930. (14)
[200] Goldsborough, Gordon and Christian Cassidy, "Memorable Manitobans: Jacob Penner," *Manitoba Historical Society* [https://www.mhs.mb.ca/docs/people/penner_j.shtml], revised September 2, 2020.
[201] "U. Students and Communists in Singing Contest," *Winnipeg Evening Tribune*, March 14, 1930. (5)
[202] "Mostly Non-Residents in Unemployed Picket Lines at Legislative Buildings," *Winnipeg Evening Tribune* July 13, 1936. (2)
[203] Thomas, A.V. "City Hall Speaking," *Winnipeg Evening Tribune*, July 14, 1936. (5)
[204] "22 Killed By heat in City as Mercury Hits New High; 9 Drowned Seeking Relief," *Winnipeg Evening Tribune*, July 13, 1936. (1)
[205] "Parade staged as protest by single jobless," *Winnipeg Evening Tribune*, May 26, 1936. (10)
[206] "Jobless Create Disturbance On Trams; Arrested," *Winnipeg Evening Tribune*, June 24,1936. (1)
[207] "Enlarge Food Hall," *Winnipeg Evening Tribune*, July 14, 1936. (4)
[208] "Council Sees Need For Better Dining Room Accommodation," *Winnipeg Evening Tribune*, July 14, 1936. (3)
[209] "Jobless jailed for refusing to pay tram fare," *Winnipeg Evening Tribune*, July 14, 1936. (3)

Chapter 6: Portage and Main Takes Centre Stage

[210] "War Savings Drive Opens" *Winnipeg Free Press*, February 7, 1941 (5)
[211] Ibid.
[212] "Boom! Boom! Boom!" *Winnipeg Evening Tribune*, June 2, 1941 (1)
[213] "Tonight's Blackout Will Be Real Battle," *Winnipeg Evening Tribune*, June 4, 1941. (1)
[214] "Here are the rules for blackout tonight" *Winnipeg Evening Tribune*, June 4, 1941. (1)
[215] It would be renamed the Childs Building in 1947.

[216] Murray, Victor Vereker 'V.V.M. Survives Without a Quiver," *Winnipeg Evening Tribune* June 5, 1941. (8).
[217] "Darkness Swallows Mammoth Crowds," *Winnipeg Free Press*, June 5, 1941. (9)
[218] "Turning Battle's Tide," *Winnipeg Evening Tribune*, February 20, 1942. (13)
[219] "Salvage Cops Plans Biggest Metal Drive" *Winnipeg Evening Tribune*, June 21, 1943. (11)
[220] Nemy, Enid V., "Winnipeg Volunteer Salvage Corps Brings in $238,000" *The Lethbridge Herald*, December 4, 1943. (8)
[221] Lepkin, Ben, "When the Good News Came…" *Winnipeg Evening Tribune*, May 7, 1945. (7)
[222] "Fund Tops 61 Percent," *Winnipeg Tribune*, October 24, 1956. (1)
[223] Smith, Graham N., "Moss I Gather," *Winnipeg Evening Tribune* August 17, 1957.
[224] Nimble Foot, "Jaywalker's Lament," *Winnipeg Evening Tribune* April 26,1951. (6)
[225]"Drive on Jaywalkers" *Winnipeg Tribune*, April 23, 1957. (1)
[226] Transit History, MHS.
[227] Julia-Simone Rutgers, "Looking back to move forward," *Winnipeg Free Press* December 29, 2023. https://www.winnipegfreepress.com/featured/2023/12/29/looking-back-to-move-forward
[228] "Alderman to Fight Boulevard," *Winnipeg Evening Tribune*. March 1, 1956. (32)
[229] "Labour Leaders Prefer Beauty Strip to New Traffic Lane," *Winnipeg Evening Tribune*, August 6, 1955. (15)
[230] "Frosh Festive as First Freshman Day Observed" *The Manitoban*, October 12, 1937. (1)
[231] "Turner Guides Galloping Godiva," *The Manitoban*, October 12, 1937. (1)
[232] "F-Day at University" *Winnipeg Free Press*, October 7, 1949. (1,3)
[233] "Welcome on Portage Halts Royal Parade," *Winnipeg Evening Tribune*, October 16, 1951. (1)
[234] "And Walkers Get Raw Deal," *Winnipeg Evening Tribune*, November 10, 1959-11-10. (15)
[235] Martz, Fraidie and Andrew Wilson, *A Fiery Soul: The Life and Theatrical Times of John Hirsch* (Montreal; Vechicule Press, 2011). (79)
[236] Ibid, 86.
[237] Morris, Frank "Here There and Hollywood" *Winnipeg Free Press* September 11, 1957. (13)
[238] Hirsch, 119.

Chapter 7: Closing the Corner

[239] Walker, David, *The Great Winnipeg Dream* (Mosaic Press; Winnipeg, Manitoba), 1979. (36)
[240] "The City of Tomorrow," *Winnipeg Tribune*, October 11, 1968. (41)
[241] Luckily for The Manitoba Theatre Centre, Winnipeg's construction boom also included developing a new arts complex across the street from City Hall.
[242] "The West's Largest Windbreak," *Winnipeg Tribune*, September 9, 1969. (23)
[243] Magnus, Dudley, "Winnipeg Inn Lays Down Law to Staff" *Winnipeg Free Press* September 10, 1970. (67)
[244] Paul Grescoe, "The Merchandising Mayor," *Winnipeg Tribune* August 13, 1977. (106)
[245] "Metro Gets the Needle," *Winnipeg Tribune,* November 17, 1965. (2)
[246] McGarry, Michael, "Mayor Juba is Cooking Up A Graham Wafer," *Winnipeg Tribune*, April 18, 1968. (1)
[247] McGarry, "Airborne Shopping Mall," *Winnipeg Tribune*, April 18, 1968. (2)
[248] Walker, *Great Winnipeg Dream*. (70)
[249] Jones, Mel "City to buy parking sites" *Winnipeg Tribune*, July 28, 1970. (1)

[250] Werier, Val, "Largest Landlord comes to town, *Winnipeg Tribune*, June 15, 1973. (6)
[251] Werier, "Great Chance at No 1 Corner," *Winnipeg Tribune* March 18, 1971. (6)
[252] Werier, "Support for the Portage Plaza," *Winnipeg Tribune* March 24, 1971. (6)
[253] "Trizec Agreement Unnecessary and Gamble," *Winnipeg Free Press*, January 23, 1974. (61)
[254] "Trizec Demolition Contact Awarded," *Winnipeg Free Press*, October 18, 1973. (28)
[255] Rostecki, Randy, "Reader Questions New Development," *Winnipeg Tribune* June 30, 1972. (1)
[256] Kustra, Ron, "Environmental Impact Studies Current Issue" *Winnipeg Tribune* December 28, 1974. (20)
[257] "A New Downtown" *Winnipeg Free Press*, November 6, 1975. (85)
[258] "Facelift for Trizec," *Winnipeg Evening Tribune* April 13, 1976. (4)
[259] Christie, Alan, "Handling Development" *Winnipeg Free Press*, January 10, 1976. (34)
[260] Kustra, "Underground is the Right Word," *Winnipeg Tribune*, September 13, 1975. (13)
[261] "City Set for Showdown on Trizec," *Winnipeg Free Press*, May 29, 1976. (3)
[262] Drabble, John, "Plastic Garage Door Foils 'Smashing' Christening," November 25, 1978 (5).
[263] CBC Archives. "That time Winnipeg closed Portage and Main to pedestrians." 1979. https://www.cbc.ca/player/play/video/1.4855419
[264] Werier, Val "Classic Twentieth Century Ugly" *Winnipeg Tribune* April 11, 1978 (8).
[265] "Out of sight, out of mind?" *Winnipeg Tribune*, February 22, 1979. (8)
[266] Smith, Chris, "Protest March Met by Cheers" *Winnipeg Tribune*, March 10, 1979. (5)
[267] "Militant Pedestrians attack new style Winnipeg intersection," *Lethbridge Herald*, April 26, 1979. (28)
[268] Ibid.
[269] Campbell, Ron, "Trizec Tower Opens" *Winnipeg Free Press* July 25, 1980 (3).

Chapter 8: Making an Icon

[270] McIlroy, Randal, "Cummings show too short on music and too long on comedy attempts," *Winnipeg Free Press* November 6, 1979. (37)
[271] Welch, Mary Agnes Welch "Portage and Main reopens after NHL kickoff" *Winnipeg Free Press*, May 31, 2011.
[272] McIlroy, Randal, "Cummings show too short on music and too long on comedy attempts," *Winnipeg Free Press*, November 5,1979(37).
[273] Randy Bachman, *Randy Bachman's Vinyl Tap Stories* (Toronto; Viking, Canada 2011). (2)
[274] Einarson, John and Randy Bachman, *Randy Bachman: Takin' Care of Business* (Toronto: McArthur & Co, 2000). (413)
[275] Gray, James H., "Winnipeg B-R-R-R-R," *Macleans* September 15, 1947. (24)
[276] "After Five Years—This," *Winnipeg Evening Tribune*, April 23, 1945. (26)
[277] "As You Like It," *Winnipeg Free Press Evening Bulletin*, January 19, 1926. (11)
[278] "Winnipeg Citizens Devoted to Extolling City's Wonders," *The Montreal Star*, October 7, 1955. (2)
[279] Kossar, Leon, "Who Says It's Cold Here" *Winnipeg Evening Tribune* January 20, 1954. (1)
[280] Werier, "Wind tests at Portage and Main," January 14, 1971 (6).
[281] Singh, J. (2018, July 1). NDP Statement on Canada Day. NDP. https://www.ndp.ca/news/ndp-statement-canada-day-0
[282] Niigaan Sinclair, "A decade of high expectations, broken promises for Indigenous peoples," *Winnipeg Free Press* January 2, 2020. https://www.winnipegfreepress.com/local/2020/01/02/a-de-

cade-of-high-expectations-broken-promises-for-indigenous-peoples
[283] Erik Pindera, "We are human, not trash," *Winnipeg Free Press* April 28, 2023 (A3)

Chapter 9: To Open or Not to Open

[284] Mary Agnes Welch, "Big order, big corner," *Winnipeg Free Press*, December 3, 2003 (p.B1-B2)
[285] Ibid.
[286] Wins Bridgman, interview by author, February 14, 2025.
[287] Mary Agnes Welch, "Big order, big corner," *Winnipeg Free Press*, December 3, 2003 (p.B1-B2)
[288] City Crossing, "City Crossing Brief" (http://winnipeg-design-competition.org/brief/city_obligations.htm); archived at *Wayback Machine* on August 4, 2004.
[289] Bridgman, interview.
[290] City Crossing, "City Brief"
[291] Wins Bridgman, "Street cred," *Winnipeg Free Press*, January 24, 2004. (p.G3)
[292] Cohlmeyer Architects Limited, "The Republic of Portage and Main," (http://winnipeg-design-competition.org/exhibition/entries/entry_19.htm); archived at *Wayback Machine* on August 4, 2004.
[293] Cohlmeyer Architects, "Republic of Portage and Main"
[294] Cohlmeyer Architects, "Republic of Portage and Main"
[295] Bridgman, interview
[296] Doug Corbett, interview with the author, February 14, 2025.
[297] Janet Rosenberg + Associates and Corbett Cibinel Architects, "Light Forest," (http://winnipeg-design-competition.org/exhibition/entries/entry_73.htm); archived at *Wayback Machine* on August 4, 2004.
[298] Janet Rosenberg and Corbett Cibinel, "Light Forest"
[299] Corbett, interview.
[300] Corbett, interview.
[301] Santin, Aldo, "Katz says barriers stay," *Winnipeg Free Press*, July 7, 2004. (p.B1-B2)
[302] Ibid.
[303] Forest, Paul, "Bring down the barriers," *Winnipeg Free Press*, July 16, 2004 (p.A11); Bruneau, Jay "Common sense brought to city hall," *Winnipeg Free Press*, September 17, 2004. (A13)
[304] Santin, Aldo, "Katz says barriers stay," *Winnipeg Free Press*, July 7, 2004. (p.B1-B2)
[305] Ibid.
[306] Alison Mayes, "'Light Forest' Awarded," *Winnipeg Free Press*, February 28, 2005. (p.B1)
[307] Reynolds, Lindor, "Removing barricades no cure-all," *Winnipeg Free Press*, March 16, 2005.
[308] Walsh, Mary Agnes, "Intersection," *Winnipeg Free Press*, March 8, 2005. (A4)
[309] Santin, Aldo, "Portage & Main makeover?" *Winnipeg Free Press*, July 6, 2004. (p.A1, A4)
[310] City of Winnipeg, "Light Forest Feasibility Study: Winnipeg City Crossing," Summer 2006.
[311] Kives, Bartley "At Cross Purposes," *Winnipeg Free Press* July 14, 2007. (p.F2)
[312] Corbett, interview.
[313] Brian Bowman (@BrianTDBowman), Twitter, August 11, 2014.
[314] Glowacki, Laura, "Portage and Main changes a 'vanity project' for Brian Bowman, says rival," *CBC News*, July 17, 2018.
[315] Kives, Bartley, "Bowman calls city director 'inaccurate' as Portage & Main confusion mounts," *CBC News*, November 30, 2016.
[316] Kives, Bartley, "Mayor wants Portage and Main open before Canada Summer Games," *CBC*

News, June 3, 2016.

[317] Brian Bowman (@BrianTDBowman) Twitter, October 13, 2017.

[318] Brian Bowman (@BrianTDBowman), Twitter, October 13, 2017.

[319] "Would have been a step backwards': Winnipeggers vote to keep Portage and Main closed," *CBC News,* October 24, 2018.

[320] "Familiar stances in debate on opening Portage and Main," *Winnipeg Free Press*, June 18, 2015, (2).

[321] Aldo Santon, "Councillor worries Portage and Main project is done deal," *Winnipeg Free Press*, September 21, 2017. (17)

[322] Sanders, Carol, "Intersection reopening jumps council hurdle," *Winnipeg Free Press*, October 26, 2017. (1)

[323] Lett, Dan, "Browaty-led bullying won the battle, but…Portage and Main war will rage on," *Winnipeg Free Press*, October 26, 2018. (pB1)

[324] Brent Bellamy, interview with Author, February 14, 2015.

[325] "Get the Facts About Portage and Main," Vote Open https://www.voteopenwpg.ca/the-facts/ (accessed March 21, 2025).

[326] Jane's Walk, https://janeswalk.org/, accessed March 27, 2025.

[327] Kives, Bartley Kives, "'Deep, intense dislike for this idea' of opening Portage and Main, poll finds," *CBC News*, September 11, 2018.

[328] Probe Research, "Winnipeggers' Views on Portage & Main," August 2018, p.6, p.20.

[329] Probe Research, "Winnipeggers' Views on Portage & Main," August 2018, p.6, p.7-8.

[330] Kives, Bartley, "'Deep, intense dislike for this idea' of opening Portage and Main, poll finds," *CBC News*, September 11, 2018.

[331] Ibid

[332] "'Would have been a step backwards': Winnipeggers vote to keep Portage and Main closed," *CBC News,* October 24, 2018.

[333] Ibid.

[334] Ibid.

[335] City of Winnipeg, "Appendix D – Survey Results," in Portage and Main Revitalization Study, 2023, https://engage.winnipeg.ca/portageandmain (accessed March 21, 2025).

[336] City of Winnipeg, "Survey Results"

[337] Probe Research, "Six in Ten Winnipeggers Support Re-Opening Portage and Main," March 21, 2024.

[338] Bellamy, interview

[339] Scott Gillingham, interview with the author, January 31, 2025.

[340] Bridgman, interview

[341] Gillingham, interview

Bibliography

Bachman, Randy. *Randy Bachman's Vinyl tap stories.* Toronto: Viking Canada. 2011.

Baker, John E. *Winnipeg's electric transit: the story of Winnipeg's streetcars and trolley busses.* Toronto, Ont: Railfare Enterprises. 1982.

Begg, Alexander and Walter R. Nursey. *Ten Years in Winnipeg: A narration of the principal events in the History of the City of Winnipeg.* Winnipeg: Times Printing and Publishing House, 1879.

Begg, Alexander. *Red River Journal and other papers relative to the Red River Resistance of 1869-1870.* Toronto: Champlain Society, 1956.

Bellamy, Brent and Barrie Ottenbreit. "City Crossing Design Winnipeg 2004." http://winnipeg-design-competition.org/exibition/entries/entry_07.htm Archived at Wayback Machine on August 4, 2004.

Bellamy, Brent. Interview with the author. February 14, 2025.

Bercuson, David Jay. *Confrontation at Winnipeg: Labour, Industrial Relations, and the General Strike.* Montreal & Kingston: McGill-Queen's University Press, 1990.

Blanchard, Jim. *A Diminished Roar.* Winnipeg: University of Manitoba Press, 2019.

Blanchard, Jim. *Thinking Big: A History of the Winnipeg Business Community to the Second World War.* Winnipeg: Great Plains, 2021.

Blanchard, Jim. *Winnipeg 1912.* Winnipeg: University of Manitoba Press, 2005.
Bradley, Walter E. "A History of Transportation in Winnipeg," *Manitoba Historical Society Transactions* Series 3, 1958-59.

Brandon Sun

Bridgman, Wins. Interview by author. February 14, 2025.

Bryce, George. "Early Days in Winnipeg." *MHS Transactions* 1, no. 46 (February 1894).

Campbell, Ron. "Environmental Impact Reviews are serious business." *Winnipeg Free Press,* March 8, 1975 (107).

Canada Department of Justice, Research and Statistics "Missing and Murdered Indigenous Women and Girls." July 2017. https://www.justice.gc.ca/eng/rp-pr/jr/jf-pf/2017/docs/july04.pdf

Canada General Statistics Branch. The Canada Yearbook 1934-35. Ottawa: J.O. Patenaude, 1935.

Cassidy, Christian. "Seven Stories about Portage and Main" *West End Dumplings*. https://westenddumplings.blogspot.com/2012/06/seven-stories-about-portage-and-main.html

Cassidy, Christian. "When Portage Avenue was known as Queen Street," *Winnipeg Free Press*, January 4, 2022.

Carter, Sarah. "KĀ-KĪWISTĀHĀW (Kahkewistahaw)." *Dictionary of Canadian Biography*, vol. 13. 1994.

CBC Archives. "When the wind chill factor got 'complicated'." December 22, 2021. https://www.cbc.ca/archives/wind-chill-explainer-1979-1.6293022

CBC Archives. "That time Winnipeg closed Portage and Main to pedestrians." 1979. https://www.cbc.ca/player/play/video/1.4855419

CBC News.

City Crossing. "City Crossing Brief." http://winnipeg-design-competition.org/brief/city_obligations.htm Archived at *Wayback Machine* on August 4, 2004.

City of Winnipeg. "Appendix D – Survey Results." In *Portage and Main Revitalization Study*, 2023. https://engage.winnipeg.ca/portageandmain Accessed March 21, 2025.

City of Winnipeg. "Light Forest Feasibility Study: Winnipeg City Crossing." Summer 2006.

Civic Social and Athletic Association. *Winnipeg— Know Our City: Souvenir of Winnipeg's Jubilee 1874-1924*. Winnipeg: West Canada Publishing Co., 1924.

Cohlmeyer Architects Limited. "The Republic of Portage and Main." http://winnipeg-design-competition.org/exhibition/entries/entry_19.htm Archived at *Wayback Machine* on August 4, 2004.

Construction: a journal for the architectural engineering and contracting interests of Canada, [Vol. 3, no. 2 (Dec. 1909)].

Corbett, Doug. Interview with the author. February 14, 2025.

Craig, Irene. "Grease Paint on the Prairies: An Account of the Theatres, the Plays, and the Players of Winnipeg from 1866 to 1921." *MHS Transactions* Series 3, April 1947.
Darragh, Brian K. *The Streetcars of Winnipeg—Our Forgotten Heritage.* Manitoba; FriesenPress, 2015.

District of Assiniboia General Quarterly Court, 1863-1872. Council of Assiniboia Fonds, P7538/3, Provincial Archives of Manitoba.

Einarson, John and Randy Bachman. *Randy Bachman, takin' care of business.* Toronto: McArthur & Co. 2000.

Elliott, George B. *Winnipeg As It Is in 1874 and As It Was in 1860.* Ottawa: Free Press, 1875.

Garrioch, Rev. A.C. *First Furrows: A History of the Early Settlement of the Red River Country, including that of Portage la Prairie*. Winnipeg: Stovel Company Limited, 1923.

Gillingham, Scott. Interview with the author. January 31, 2025.

Goundry, Pam. "Worked Shell" in *A 3000-Year-Old Native Campsite and Trade Centre at The Forks*. Winnipeg: The Forks Public Archaeology Association, compiled by Sid Kroker and Pam Goundry, 1993 pp192-199, 205.

Goundry, Pam. *The Heritage Beneath Our Feet.* Winnipeg: The Forks North Portage Partnership, 2002.

Gray, James H. *The Winter Years: The Depression on the Prairies*. Calgary: Fifth House Ltd, 2003.

Hargrave, Joseph James. *Red River.* Montreal: Printed by John Lovell, 1871.

Hartman, James B. "On Stage: Theatre and Theatres in Early Winnipeg." *Manitoba History*. Number 43, Spring / Summer 2002

Hartman, James B. "The Churches of Early Winnipeg." *Manitoba History* 45 (Spring/Summer 2003).

Healy, W.J. *Winnipeg's Early Days*. Stovel Company Ltd.: Winnipeg, Manitoba. 1927.

Historical Buildings Committee. "335 Main Street: The Bank of Montreal". City of Winnipeg. Historical Buildings Committee: Winnipeg, MB. (1980).

Illustrated Souvenir of Winnipeg (W.A. Martel and Sons; Winnipeg, Manitoba). 1903.

Interviews with Allan Sutherland and Niigaan Sinclair for One Great History, 2023.

Janet Rosenberg + Associates and Corbett Cibinel Architects. "Light Forest." http://winnipeg-design-competition.org/exhibition/entries/entry_73.htm Archived at *Wayback Machine* on August 4, 2004.

Kirbyson, Geoff. *The Hot Line: How the Legendary Trio of Hull, Hedberg and Nilsson Transformed Hockey and Led the Winnipeg Jets to Greatness.* Great Plains Press; Winnipeg, Manitoba 2016.

Kramer, Reinhold and Tom Mitchell, *When the State Trembled*. Toronto: University of Toronto Press, 2010.

Kustra, Ron. "Environmental impact studies current issue." *Winnipeg Tribune* December 28. 1974 (20)

La Liberté

Levine, Allan. *The Exchange: 100 Years of Trading Grain in Winnipeg* Winnipeg: Peguis Publishers Limited, 1987.

Lewycky, Dennis. *Magnificent Fight: The 1919 General Strike*. Halifax & Winnipeg: Fernwood Publishing, 2019.

MacBeth, R.G. *Sir Augustus Nanton: A Biography*. Toronto: MacMillan, 1931.

Martz, Fraidie, and Andrew Wilson. *A Fiery Soul: The Life and Theatrical Times of John Hirsch.* (Montreal; Vechicule Press). 2011.

McIntyre, Mike. "Hockey hall of fame, human hall of shame" *Winnipeg Free* Press January 30, 2023.

Morning Telegram

Nanton, Paul. "A.M. Nanton's 41 Years in Winnipeg, 1883-1924." *Manitoba History* 6 (Fall 1983).

Nanton, Paul. *Prairie Explosion: Setting the Pace for Canada.* Canada, Nanton Press, 2010.

Naylor, James, Rhonda L. Hinther, and Jim Mochoruk, eds. *For a Better World: The Winnipeg General Strike & The Workers' Revolt.* Winnipeg: University of Manitoba Press, 2022.

Paul, Alexandra. "In Praise of Peguis," *Winnipeg Free Press*, July 15, 2017.

Perrun, Jody. *The Patriotic Consensus: Unity, Morale, and the Second World War in Winnipeg* Winnipeg, MB; University of Manitoba Press). 2014.

Pinsent, Gordon. *By The Way*. Stoddart; Canada, 1992.

Probe Research. "Six in Ten Winnipeggers Support Re-Opening Portage and Main." March 21, 2024.

Probe Research. "Winnipeggers' Views on Portage & Main." August 2018.

Reynolds, George F. "The Man Who Created the Corner of Portage and Main." *MHS Transaction* 3, no. 26 (1969-70).

Ronaghan, Neil Edgar. "The Archibald Administration in Manitoba 1870-1872." PhD Dissertation, University of Manitoba, 1987.

Rostecki, R.R. *Portage and Main: A Short History.* City of Winnipeg Historical Buildings Committee, 2003.

Rostecki, Randy R. "Some Old Winnipeg Buildings." *MHS Transactions* (Series 3, Number 29), 1972-73.

Rutgers, Julia-Simone. "Looking back to move forward." *Winnipeg Free Press*. December 29, 2023. https://www.winnipegfreepress.com/featured/2023/12/29/looking-back-to-move-forward

Sinclair, Gordon Jr. "The Prince and the Paper" *Winnipeg Free Press*, May 12, 2012.

Sinclair, Niigaan. "Smallpox epidemic left massive Indigenous burial ground under Winnipeg's downtown." *Winnipeg Free Press*. October 2, 2018.

Smith, Chris. "In this corner, new challenger for windy title" *Winnipeg Tribune* January 28, 1980.1980.

Smith, Doug. *Joe Zuken: Citizen and Socialist* (James Lorimer and Company; Toronto). 1990.

Smith, Doug. *Let Us Rise! An Illustrated History of the Manitoba Labour Movement.* Winnipeg: Public Press, 1985.

Spector, David. "Monuments to Finance: Three Winnipeg Banks," report by City of Winnipeg Historical Buildings Committee: Winnipeg, MB. (1980).

Teillet, Jean. *The North-West is Our Mother: The Story of Louis Riel's People, the Métis Nation.* Toronto, Ontario, Canada: HarperCollins Publishers, 2019.

The New Nation

The Nor'Wester, "Important Statement of Pegowis Indian Chief," October 14, 1863 (3).

The Voice

Thorsteinson, Jeffrey. "Public Art" *Winnipeg Architecture Foundation*. 2014.

Thorsteinson, Jeffrey. "*Mallifying the "Crossroads of the West": How Portage and Main Went Underground.* Society for the Study of Architecture in Canada. December 17, 2020. https://canada-architecture.org/mallifying-the-crossroads-of-the-west-how-portage-and-main-went-underground/

Walker, David C. *The Great Winnipeg Dream* (Mosaic Press; Winnipeg, Manitoba). 1979.

Wasney, Eva. "Digging up hope for massive art below Portage and Main" *Winnipeg Free Press*, March 7, 2024.

Western Labor News

Winnipeg Daily Sun

Winnipeg Free Press

Winnipeg Royal Welcome Week Committee, "Happy and glorious: A cavalcade of welcome – Winnipeg Royal Welcome Week Committee," 1939. Courtesy of Peels Prairie Provinces. https://archive.org/details/N021552/

Winnipeg Telegram

Winnipeg Tribune, "Golden Memories - souvenir booklet of the 1939 Royal Visit to Canada", 1939. Courtesy of Peels Prairie Provinces. https://archive.org/details/golden-memories/

Winnipeg Tribune